1.75

Purity
and
Power

Purity and Power

Keswick Ministry
from Dick Lucas, Alan Flavelle,
Philip Hacking, David Jackman
& others

Edited by David Porter

STL Books

PO Box 48, Bromley, Kent, England
PO Box 28, Waynesboro, Georgia 30830, USA

Keswick Convention Council, England

© 1981 The Keswick Convention Council

STL Books are published by Send The Light Trust,
9 London Road, Bromley, Kent, England.

All rights reserved. No part of this publication may be
reproduced, stored in a retrieval system, or transmitted, in
any form or by any means, electronic, mechanical,
photocopying, recording or otherwise without the prior
permission of the Keswick Convention Council.

ISBN 0 903843 59 5

Cover photograph by courtesy
of British Tourist Authority

Made and printed by
Hunt Barnard Printing, Aylesbury, Bucks.

CONTENTS

INTRODUCTION

by Canon A S Neech
(Chairman of the Keswick Convention Council)

Some of the worst riots ever seen on British streets took place in Brixton and Liverpool just before the Keswick Conventions were held this year and some of these addresses refer to them. Keswick itself had a similar devastating experience when a thousand motor cycling youngsters went on the rampage at the lakeside on the Saturday night after the Convention had finished. What worlds apart they were from the thousands of young people who heard these addresses and others not included here. They had come to hear Keswick's traditional emphasis on the scriptural call for purity and the secret of power for Christian living through God's indwelling Spirit. And they did not just hear, they responded with a complete dedication of heart and life to Christ their Lord.

Personal purity and the individual's experience of God's grace and power are one side of Keswick's emphasis. To leave them as a purely personal matter is to deny New Testament teaching. Individuals make up churches and nations. God's concern is for His church and the world and this must be our concern too.

This year's ministry, once again, faithfully maintained this scriptural balance. Keswick is not a holy huddle of people escaping from the world. They are there to learn how to be more effective in it.

During each week questionnaires were distributed and

among other things they revealed that the proportion of young people present was surprisingly and gratifyingly high. More than half of all those present had never been before. People who live and work in nearly sixty different countries were there. For them they were two marvellous weeks of fellowship and teaching. As you read these pages you will see why. Do not read too much at a time. Really make your own what you read and put into practice all that you learn.

Here are strong words of encouragement and hope for every human situation. The Bible is like that, always practical, everywhere relevant, God's timely word for all our needs. Keswick 1981 proved it again as you will agree as you read these stimulating pages now.

EDITOR'S INTRODUCTION

Perhaps your editor is getting a little long in the tooth on the job, but it did seem an awfully difficult task this year. The cutting and pasting was necessary, to produce the book you hold in your hands; but it was no fun abbreviating this year's ministry. In almost every case much of what was omitted would very likely have been retained by another editor, and certainly by this one if space had been unlimited. The consolation is that what has been included is material of such value as to make this volume a vintage Keswick report,

The choice of what is included is the Keswick Council's (made on the basis of how the addresses were received at Keswick). Working on the book was, as it always is, a rare spiritual privilege; and many of the words which were left out of the edited version were words which spoke to me, and presumably many others, in a direct and personal way. I hope you will agree, however, that the flavour and content of the addresses included come over. For the full, uncut versions you must make use of the excellent tape library facilities mentioned elsewhere in this book.

This year, we have included addresses which relate to each other, to illustrate how different speakers endorsed and built on what others had said, and so once again manifested that extraordinary unanimity of thought which characterises the Convention. Thus Dr Raymond Brown's study of Uzziah follows Rev David Jackman's address on 'Road blocks' in the book, just as it did on the evening of 13 July at Keswick; and Canon James Ayre refers back to Rev Sinclair Ferguson's study of Demas given the previous day. The most remarkable instance in the book of harmony between speakers is shown in the last address of all, given by Rev Chuck Smith following Canon Ayre's exposition of the first half of Psalm 73. So gripped was he by the theme that he abandoned his prepared address and spoke extempore on the second half of the Psalm, in the address which concludes this book.

(Chuck Smith should certainly be mentioned in any account of Keswick 1981; he exerted an almost Pied-Piper-like appeal towards young people, whose meetings he led during the first week. He also gave several Convention addresses. Pastor of a church in America with an extraordinary history and a gigantic congregation, his opening of the Word of God spoke in a personal way to many who came to Keswick.)

The editorial practice in this book is the same as in previous years. The intention has been to preserve as much of the original as possible without paraphrasing the speaker's words. This has meant the loss of some telling illustrations, some extended Bible quotations, and some good jokes. The Bible studies are in general less heavily edited than the addresses.

As regards Bible references, we have followed our usual method; we have assumed that the readers will have an open Bible in front of them, just as the speakers assumed that their listeners would in the tent. We have not included all references in full (though nearly all appear at least in part), and we have not always indicated where a speaker is paraphrasing. Where a straight quotation is given, this has been checked against the appropriate version.

In reading this report, bear in mind that the speakers have graciously waived the right of scrutiny of the edited text, in order to speed publication. The book must therefore be seen as an edited transcript of spoken ministry, not as a polished, reworked and thoroughly checked literary work. No attempt has been made to remove the characteristics of the spoken word, though some of the more immediate references to Keswick, the tent and its surroundings have been removed.

Finally, I and the Keswick Council would wish to record our thanks to the army of voluntary typists who transcribed tapes and thus provided the raw material of the book. I would on my own account also wish to thank Charles Cartwright of Liss Forest, whose technical skills on certain complicated equipment twice rescued the editorial schedule from disaster.

David Porter

THE BIBLE READINGS

THE PURITY OF THE CHURCH

by Rev Dick Lucas

1. The Impurity of the Church and the Anger of God

We're going to turn to what has been called the most neglected letter in the New Testament. It's just one slim page; a book of one chapter, twenty-five verses. I think it would be true to say that for many of us (and especially for younger Christians) this book is hardly known. Indeed I would go so far as to say that most of us know only one or two verses. But those are known by nearly everybody; those wonderful words of the closing doxology, verses 24, 25.

However, it isn't just those two verses which are inspired; all Scripture is given by inspiration of God, and none of it may safely be neglected. It's true that Jude may not be regarded as the staple diet of the Christian church – it's not one of the great New Testament books like Romans or Revelation – nevertheless, it is a letter which (like all these smaller letters) is of vital importance in special times. And I believe that just such a time is with us now, when this book speaks to us especially powerfully.

If I were to give this series of Bible readings a title it would be: *The Purity of the Church*. We read in Ephesians 5:27 that Christ gave Himself for the Church, to present her to Himself as a perfect, clean, holy, unblemished bride. That is His purpose; He will do it whether we like it or not – as the last verses of Jude show us. It is His purpose. Whatever it costs, His bride is going to be pure.

Verses 1, 2: Brother Jude

So then to this little letter about the purity of the Church. I
want to begin with just a few words about brother Jude.

First of all, his home. There is only one pair of brothers
called James and Jude mentioned in the New Testament, so
it is I think a safe assumption that this is the Jude mentioned
in Mark 6. We know nothing more about him than what we
see through that brief window into his home. It is significant,
however, that somebody who had grown up in that family
should, when he was grown up and held a position of
leadership in the Church, be concerned about questions of
purity and holiness. He'd seen it lived before him, you see, in
his home.

Secondly, his conversion. We know nothing of how or
when Jude came to see Jesus in a new way – not as a brother,
but as his Lord. But we see from those introductory verses
that it had happened. And it must have been very
remarkable, must it not? Because we are told that the
brothers of Jesus, before His resurrection, did not believe in
Him; and yet here we are told that Jude has become a servant
of Jesus Christ.

Thirdly, his authority. Notice that he calls himself a
brother of James. It is not (as some have suggested) a way of
demonstrating his modesty, contrasting his servitude to
Christ to his brotherhood with James. After the resurrection, nobody would have expected the old relationship of
'brother of Jesus' to have been the same; we read that in the
Gospels. It is very unlikely that Jude would ever have been
tempted to refer even negatively to the fact that he was Jesus'
brother. No; he refers to James because he wants to identify
himself with the authority of the church in Jerusalem, with
that great Christian leader James. And he calls himself a
servant of Jesus Christ to emphasise that what he says comes
from God; he has the authority of his master. So these two
sentences taken together demonstrate Jude's authority and
claim the right to be heard.

Fourthly, and briefly, his hold on God. What a doctrine of
God he has! His hold on God is shown by his understanding

of the hold God had on him and on the Church. Don't you sometimes cringe, as you get older as a Christian, at the way some Christians say: 'God will do this or that – if you let Him ... the Holy Spirit is waiting for you to allow Him to do this or that ...' A funny doctrine of God and of the Holy Spirit, that! It's not the God of the Bible. God takes the initiative, He chooses us; and so Jude writes to those who are 'called, beloved and kept'. All the emphasis is upon what God has done and is doing.

Now it is true that Jude, like all the New Testament writers, walks on two legs and doesn't hop along on one. And in verse 21, as we shall see, he lays a responsibility upon us to 'keep ourselves in the love of God'. But there you see is the balance. It would be impossible for me to keep myself, if I were not sure that God is keeping me. Like a good pastor, before he warns his people, before he warns them that the ground is in danger of opening up under their feet, he tells them that there is a God who knows all about it and goes before them. So Jude is known for his hold on God. He is confident that God is a holding, a keeping God.

Two more little things about Jude. He is completely at home in the Old Testament; quotations come readily to his mind, he mentions a name and expects you to pick it up. He writes to a people grounded in the Old Testament, and he expects his readers to know it well. And also, he is familiar with the world of nature, as you will see in verse 12. Perhaps several in that home in Nazareth loved nature and used it in their teachings. Certainly Jesus did, and James, and so did Jude. He was an acute observer of the skies, the waves and the trees.

Verse 4: An emergency situation

Let's read then verse 4, in which Jude tells us the emergency situation which has arisen. Certain men have 'wormed their way in' to the churches, as one modern translation puts it. They are now influential leaders and teachers in this group of churches to which Jude writes (although this has been called the universal catholic epistle, almost certainly Jude had particular churches in mind). I'm not going to say too much about them now because in our next Bible reading I want to try to build up an 'identikit picture' of them – because I think it's very important that we should recognise these people today. For the present, let one word from verse 4 suffice. They are 'ungodly' persons; by which Jude means that they are unspiritual and unregenerate. They are not converted Christian men; but they are becoming influential in what they say and do in the churches. It's quite an eye-opener, isn't it? In the latter part of the first century, in churches founded by apostles, already ungodly men are entering in and bringing about an emergency situation.

Obviously this must have been due to some extent to slack discipline, just as it is today in the churches of the West, indeed in the churches of the whole world. We can only speak of the denominations to which we belong; I'm an Anglican, and the confessional standard of my church is the Thirty-nine Articles, one of the fruits of the Reformation. When I was ordained you had to swear your allegiance to these articles, as setting the limits to Christian belief if you were going to be a leader and a minister in the Christian Church. And I remember the shock it was to me even thirty years ago to see men willing to sign that document, the Thirty-nine Articles before them, with a smile and a shrug of the shoulders, and the bishop winking at the fact that they didn't believe it, they weren't going to stand by it. And I'm afraid that this has so often become the case. Now you may argue about the particular confession that is needed; but I think one thing must be said, that if you have any standard at all, you must take it seriously; otherwise it becomes a mockery.

I have on my shelves at home a book called *The Climate of Treason*, the story of how certain undergraduates at Cambridge in the thirties were infiltrated by Communism. It was a godless time in our country; the Christian faith seems to have been weak in our universities. And so many of these men took up Communism almost as a new religion. They ultimately infiltrated our secret services, and everybody knows the story of Burgess, Maclean and Philby. It was impossible for their fellow men, coming from the same social background, to believe that these men could be unpatriotic. And so for years they went on doing their work against our country. It's an astonishing story. It puts James Bond in the shade. It seems unbelievable that they were never detected.

Now although that sounds melodramatic language, there has been a climate of treason in the Church for most of this century. It's a shock to talk like this. It seems ungentlemanly to talk in this way about our fellow-ministers, our fellow-leaders. And it must have been a shock in the first century, too; that's why in verse 4 Jude says that they were 'long ago designated for this condemnation' – God hasn't been taken by surprise; the people are not to panic and feel that God has left the Church because this is happening. But that the presence of these men in the Church is treasonable, Jude is in no doubt at all.

Two hallmarks

In verse 4, Jude gives us two hallmarks of these men which are perpetually true and are very true today.

First, they *'pervert the grace of our God into licentiousness'*. By the grace of God Jude doesn't mean any specific doctrine. It is simple New Testament shorthand for 'the gospel'. They are perverting the very gospel itself. Colossians 1:6 – what is the gospel? It is 'the grace of God in truth'. How do you sum up the gospel in a single word? 'Power'? 'Love'? 'Faith'? The New Testament uses the word 'grace'. It's not grasped by many young converts today. And I'm hardly surprised – they hear such a thin gospel preached today, which seems to revolve around accepting Jesus Christ as Lord, that they get the impression that that's all that the gospel is. But the gospel isn't in the first place about receiving Jesus as Lord. It's about Jesus receiving you! To accept Christ is to accept the unbelievable, amazing truth that God will accept me if I come to Him – He will not cast me out. But we hear the gospel preached in such a thin way today that we often don't come to realise this until we have been a Christian for some years.

And so having come to utter despair, to a bitter realisation of our failure, we think 'Well, I give up, because God's obviously given up on me. He can't use me now, He can't have me in His family now … Now I realise how weak and faithless I am; God can't possibly deal with me now' – you've come to that position, haven't you? I hope so; it's absolutely essential, that self-discovery, before I can discover the grace of God.

And then to believe that despite what you are and have been, despite your faithlessness as a Christian, God will still deal with you, will still pick you up, dust you down, forgive you, put His Spirit upon you and use you – that's a marvel, isn't it? That's a miracle, that's grace. That's the gospel.

If you could see my heart as I speak to you now you would probably stop listening immediately and go and have a cup of coffee. If I could see yours I probably wouldn't bother to go on speaking. It's the grace of God, isn't it, that makes it possible for me to serve God, to go on teaching you the Bible and for you to listen and learn afresh of the grace of God. Grace is the very essence of the gospel. It is so wonderful, that I come to depend utterly on the grace of God.

And therein lies the danger. That I will begin to take less heed of the warnings, be less careful. It's especially easy to do this in an age when the light that is shed on the great doctrines is very weak. It's said that recent hymnbooks have fewer hymns on sin that ever before. The fear of God is hardly mentioned in many of our evangelical churches. The centre of our faith hardly seems to be Calvary any longer. No wonder, when there's a feeble light shining on sin, on the fear of God, and Calvary, that grace is barely understood and easily perverted. Because of the slackness of my own heart I begin to presume upon the divine mercy. And I begin to think that 'God is no tyrant', that though our standards of personal discipline are dropped to the point where we do things that an earlier generation of Christians would not have dreamed of doing, they were nevertheless harsh and legalistic; and I am in danger of descending to the state of that stinging word at the end of verse 4, 'licentiousness'. The Greek word is *aselgeia* -- 'shamelessness'. We were ashamed of certain things. Shame is a very valuable thing. It is a mark that we are in the presence of God; I can't do, or think, or feel certain things without feeling ashamed of myself. That's wholesome. That's what a sinner ought to feel, when he's saved by grace. If I get into a position where I'm no longer ashamed of things that displease God, then I'm in a very unwholesome position.

I do not want to mention these things, but one has to today, if one is to make plain what one is talking about. There is a minister of a church very near to me in London who has lived with another man for ten years. This homosexual relationship has been an offence to many Christian people living nearby. When recently I wrote to him because I felt it was time we were open with each other on this matter, I received back not an angry letter but a very gracious one. The letter spoke of the warm companionship over many years, the meeting of human needs, which this relationship had provided. His challenge to me was clearly this: 'Can you, as a compassionate Christian person, condemn this?'

That is how the question is so often put, is it not? And so often we can sympathise with how the temptation came. But we cannot sympathise with sin, can we? Grace must lead to godliness.

Secondly, *these men 'deny our only Master and Lord, Jesus Christ'*. This could simply mean that they professed Jesus as Lord but denied Him by their deeds. But I think it is something more than that; it is a second hallmark by which we can recognise these men, that they deny the lordship and authority of Jesus.

Turn to 1 John 2:22. It seems that at the end of the New Testament period this is the way that some of the writers spoke of the denial of Christ. There is no doubt in this verse that the denial is of doctrine – with practical implications, certainly, but there is first and foremost here a failure to recognise that God is known supremely, and only, through Jesus Christ, who is Lord, and to whom ultimate divine authority is given.

Now if this is what Jude means – and I'm almost sure it is – you will see, if you put the two hallmarks together, that they are always found together (that is why I believe I'm right in interpreting the passage in this way). You see, you can't bring in a new morality without bringing in a new theology. You've got to disparage the old authorities by which Christians have looked at things in the past, if you're going to bring in a new way of looking at things. That's obvious, isn't it. So, for example, the 'Law of God' becomes something of a dirty word. I hope you Christians know that God cannot speak without laying down the law – in that sense, everything He says is law as well as promise. Every word of God is authoritative. If He was pleased by the keeping of the Commandments in the past, He can't be pleased by the breaking of them today. We can't be free from the Law, as some have argued we can be – 'Because of the love of God we are entirely free from the Law of God' – that's absolute nonsense, and dangerous nonsense. The Law of God has the same authority on us as it always had. Not as a way of salvation, but as a pattern, a standard, of Christian holiness.

We can see from verse 25 that there was a real falling away from authority even in the early Church. The ascription to Christ of 'all authority' is a reminder that you cannot take authority away from Christ and maintain Christian standards. The authority that belongs to the deity of Christ is absolute. We cannot trade it in. Of course it is a great stumbling-block: what a stumbling block Christ is to all the great liberal evolutionary theories of knowledge there are today! It is said that we know better today; that there must be a graph of knowledge going slowly upwards; with our increased knowledge of interpersonal relationships and so forth, we know better today ... In a sense it is true. But the Christian says something which is a great stumbling-block to the humanist intellectual world. He says, 'Yes; there is a rising graph of knowledge in many things; but we go back 2,000 years. And there, on the ultimate issues of relationships, of God with man and man with God – there is the final word. And no final word has been spoken beyond it.'

Verse 3: The Christian response

So: what are the Christians to do? Are they to quit? Now that the mutineers have come on board, are they to leave the ship? I fully understand those who give such advice today, and it is often very sincerely given; because if the mutineers stay on board, the ship will sink ... All the more interesting therefore to read verse 3. Here is a great apostolic appeal. Contend! Don't abandon it to them!

I cannot give you an adequate idea here of just how strong the verb is. In our own language we add things to words to strengthen them. If we want to say something is more than abundant we say it is 'super-abundant'. Now, imagine you could add another 'super' to make 'super-super-abundant'. That gives some idea of the lengths Jude has gone to to strengthen the word he is using. It means 'to fight with every fibre of one's being'. So it means that however peaceable we are by nature (and I think that's true of most of us), however much we shrink from the battle, each one of us is, by virtue of our discipleship, committed to this battle. You cannot, and I cannot, stand on the touchline. (And Jude has had a very great effect on my own life. I've been to certain meetings and spoken on certain topics since I studied Jude that I would never have spoken on before; because I believe it commits me, as a matter of simple obedience, to contend for the faith.)

Jude does not here mean by 'the faith' – as some commentators have said – merely the 'full orthodox creed', as though this were some second-century letter. He has his eye on that great phrase in the Epistle to the Hebrews, where we read of the sacrifice made 'once for all' (9:26). Look at that chapter, and you will find that 'the faith once for all delivered' is taken up with the sacrifice once for all made. Because the Christian gospel is taken up with Calvary – because the finished work of Christ *is* the gospel – because the Church was saved there – that is the once for all faith that Jude tells us we have to contend for. Nothing needed to be added. There can be nothing more beyond that finality. 'Christ, and Him crucified' – we want nothing more than that. A divine Lord, and a Calvary-centred faith and life.

Now he appeals that we should contend for that faith. Self-denial – taking up the cross – do you hear about it in your church? I hope so. If you do, I'm so glad. Because there are people around us in the churches who are going to try to destroy the deity of Christ and destroy a Calvary-centred faith – and a Calvary-centred life.

So you see these men in Jude aren't merely curious heretics, that you burrow away in the British Museum to find the names of. Nobody's ever discovered who exactly they were, incidentally. I'm so glad. I think God in His providence has stopped us from knowing, because He wants us to apply this in every generation – there are always men like this. We are to contend for the faith.

Verses 5-7: The price of failing to contend

In the next very important section, with which we close our study, we see Jude warning the churches to which he writes of what will happen if they do not contend for the faith, if they do not stand up to these men. Three things will happen.

The first illustration (verse 5) is of the Church in the wilderness. Notice how simply these illustrations are used. Jude assumes that all the converted and baptised Christians have been fully informed about all this, right at the beginning of their Christian life. They've been told the meaning of this story. They've been told of the great liberation out of Egypt into freedom. For forgiveness is deliverance; and that great exodus stands there at that point in the Bible, throwing its light forward to that great exodus which Christ accomplished at Jerusalem.

So Jude's readers have experienced the mighty redeeming word of God in bringing them out of slavery into the liberty of the children of God. 'He who saved the people . . .' – what a wonderful sentence! Just as He's brought us out of the world, a world under judgement.

'He who saved . . . afterward destroyed.' I don't know anything more chilling in the whole of Jude than that. It is aweful in its simplicity. We're told in Numbers 14: 34, 35, that a whole generation wandered in the wilderness until it died. That was God's judgement. The people who were brought out of Egypt died and left their bodies in the wilderness. Because of their sins and unbelief, Moses was doomed to lead them round and round, back in a circle, until a whole generation died out. It's a tragic story, isn't it? It made Moses weep, because he had to bear something of that with them and died himself before crossing into the Promised Land.

Now what Jude is telling us here is that those God delivers He will destroy, if they cease to be real churches. What is a real church? We find out in the last sentence of verse 5. It's quite simple. Jude speaks of 'those who did not believe'. Here is a company of people who call themselves believers, but as God sees it they have ceased to believe, and so they have ceased to be a church. It's so simple. He destroys what is not his own. The people in the wilderness had ceased to be believers.

How do you destroy a church? We know from the story of the Church in China that you cannot do it by the most vicious attacks from outside. But what verse 5 is saying is that a church can be destroyed from within, by sin and unbelief. Look at modern Turkey. Compare it with those atlases which show the New Testament churches. I have one which shows them as little lamps, all over Asia Minor. Have you ever been to Turkey, for a holiday perhaps? What did you find? A handful of believers in Ankara. One or two here, a few there – hardly amounting to a fellowship in the whole of Turkey. All those New Testament churches snuffed out and destroyed ... were they destroyed by the power of the conqueror? Or was it through inner rot and unbelief? What was it?

You see church buildings evacuated near your church at home. Churches that have gone. Sometimes it's because of population movements – it may be wise stewardship; sometimes it's good to leave a building behind. But it may be this, could it not? The Church of Christ can never be destroyed. But churches can be destroyed; institutions, denominations can be destroyed.

Verse 6. The angels here stand for the privileged leaders. The angel has two privileges in the Bible. He stands in the presence of God (like Gabriel); he also serves the heirs of salvation (Hebrews 1: 14). He is called to have the supreme privilege given to every minister in the church; that of standing close to God and ministering to His people. Every Christian worker is called in some measure to that great privilege.

What happened was this. If you are going to servc the people of God, the elect, with love and humble ministry, you've got to live under the authority of God. But we're told that the angels in pride refused to do so and claimed an authority of their own. In sitting loose therefore to the authority of God, and taking authority to themselves, they found themselves when face to face with the people of God treating them not with love, but with lust: not ruling them, but exploiting them. It is something we see time and time again in Church history. If I will not stand close to God, recognising His authority and the fact that I am His slave and servant – if I try instead to be separate from Him, and exercise my own authority over men and rule them – it will indeed be a tyranny, for I will make men serve me. That's what's been seen in many of the churches today; people not content with the position of authority God has given them, seeking to find an authority for themselves, exploiting not only the souls but also the bodies of the people of God for their own lust. That's a terrible thing, isn't it? Something to make you tremble. We'll think further about that in our next study.

Well, then: what happens if the people of God, the local churches, cease to believe? What happens if the leaders of those churches have ceased to stand under the authority of God and are destroying the people of God through their behaviour? What happens when you've got an unbelieving local church and unfaithful leaders? Jude is fond of putting things in threes, and we would expect him to go on now to give us a picture of the culmination of this disaster. And he does.

Verse 5 stands for the people of God; verse 6 stands for

their leaders; and verse 7 stands for the society in which they live. You mustn't think of Sodom and Gomorrah as smoky cities. We read in Genesis that the Cities of the Plain looked – as our own country has so often been described – a 'green and pleasant land'. It's where you'd have wanted to spend a holiday, where you'd have been delighted to have been sent on business. 'What?' you'd have said, 'the Cities of the Plain? I'm glad to go there.' Yet there came a day when Abraham, after that wonderful intercession, calling on God to deliver His people, took that early morning walk up to the hilltop, and looked down on those fertile cities; and all he could see was smoke, 'like the smoke of a furnace' (Genesis 19:28).

The devastation of Sodom and Gomorrah is a visible thing, intended to stand as a visible example for all the Church down the ages; it has always done so in the Old Testament and so it should in the New. It is a sign that God will overthrow a green and pleasant land. He is no respecter of our heritage. He will visit a country with judgement if the church in that country has ceased to believe and its leaders have ceased to serve it.

That's the terrifying picture in the beginning of Jude. There's nothing difficult, nothing strange in this teaching; but it ought to chill us and to frighten us. Certain men have wormed their way in, Jude says; they pervert the grace of God into licentiousness, they deny the authority and the deity of Christ. And so, Jude continues, 'I want to remind you of those stories that you know so well; how God, when He saw that His people no longer believed, destroyed them; and when He saw that their leaders were no longer content with their supreme privilege of serving under His authority, He destroyed them; and in bringing about their downfall, He brought about the downfall of the society in which they lived.'

2. The Impurity of the Church and the Men Concerned

Jude's great concern, as we have seen from verse 4, is that certain men with no spiritual credentials have infiltrated into the churches almost unnoticed. We looked at some of the hallmarks of these men and the warnings in verses 5-7 (both for churches and the societies in which those churches are planted) of what will happen if these men are not recognised and dealt with.

After verse 7, you will find that Jude refers constantly to 'these men'; in verses 8, 10, 12, 16, and 19. He mentions them with a certain amount of scorn, I think, and also of alarm; he has them in his sights. And this is a clear hint to us that Jude was not written as a general letter to all churches but to certain churches where there was trouble because of particular people. And it's Jude's concern to awaken Christians to recognise who those people are, so that they can see the kind of teachers they should avoid.

We don't know today who those particular people were, and, as I said in our previous study, I'm sure that's due to God's providence and wisdom. What we need to know – and what Scripture gives us – is some recognisable hallmarks. Down the ages, in all the churches throughout the world, there is danger of 'these men' appearing again, and it's important that the saints should be alerted. We need an 'identikit picture' in our minds. The problem is that these men can be undetected for too long, until the damage is done. Only then do people wake up and see what has happened.

One more introductory word. Don't be put off by the strong colours in which Jude paints. Actually the New Testament often does that. Jude does it superbly and unforgettably, as I hope you will agree as we study his book together. It is like a self-portrait by the painter Van Gogh. You would never dream of painting your own face in startling blues, reds and yellows! But if you look at the work of the great artist, and look at those haunting eyes, those amazing insights into his own character, I tell you, it is quite gripping. I say this because people have been put off by these sentences of Jude; they've thought he is exaggerating. The one thing I'm anxious to show you is that he is not exaggerating; in a most brilliant way he's actually going to the heart of the situation every time, and as you look at these people, your reaction, I hope, will be to say: 'Ah, now I see what it is!'

Three Old Testament characters

Our key verse in this study is verse 11. I'm going to take up these three characters and the expository remarks Jude makes about them. But first I want to go back to verses 8 to 10. Verses 8 and 9, of course, link on to verses 5 and 7. Some very brief comments, but I think revealing ones, by way of introduction.

The first thing to say is that these men are very bold, and they are bold along the two lines that we saw in verse 4 – the new immorality and the new theology that they have brought into the churches. They are very bold in how they behave. They 'defile the flesh'. They were quite open about it. They seemed not to care about the old standards. And they were very bold and shocking in their unbelief, simply reviling the great truths that everybody else had revered. They were daring in word and deed, and in fact in their deeds (he says in verse 10) they were beastly. They were like irrational animals.

This is very true to experience. At first sight it may seem

strange, especially perhaps to the older generation. But I want to illustrate it by looking at some young person from a good, orthodox Christian home, who has entered university or college. You come from a church where people would be rather shocked if you questioned the things that the pastor taught. In that church nothing is ever questioned. It's taken for granted that what the Bible says is true and what the pastor teaches is true and the lives people live are holy and good and cannot possibly be questioned according to the Word of God; and that's right.

Of course universities or colleges are places where there are – and must be – questions. But there comes the danger; especially in Religious Studies, when you go into the lecture room and you find these things are questioned. And not just questioned in order to bring you to firmer conviction, but fearlessly, scornfully attacked. So all the things you hold precious are regarded as a kind of 'tame conformity', an unquestioned orthodoxy which you must put out of your mind completely now, if you're going to think properly.

Far from this being horrifying (though it may be so at first), I want to tell you that it can sometimes seem rather exciting. It can, for the young untrained mind, be thrilling; here is a man who doesn't dare to take for granted things that everybody at home has always taken for granted. He simply throws them to the winds! And the impression he gives of the old folks at home is that they're behind the times – they just haven't moved! All this sounds tremendously exciting. It seems as though this new teacher is unafraid to question old assumptions; and we must follow him.

There are two devastating touches to this little paragraph. The phrase 'their dreamings' (verse 8) is an important one. Jude is not talking about erotic dreams and their uncleanness. He's talking about dreams as one of the main means of revelation in the Old Testament. It could be that he is saying that 'these men' were visionaries and claimed that their visions came from God. But what is more important for us, I think, is that they were saying that God was revealing these things to them, you could depend on them because they knew what God was saying, the Spirit was leading them into new truth. Other people didn't understand, but they did, and they could teach you. And they said it with such sweeping statements, in such bold colours, that people, especially the young, were carried away.

They said God had taught them. They said the Church was being led on towards these things, that we must put the cobwebs back where they belong. And what does Jude say of them? Well, in verse 10, he says: 'They do not understand'. Quite plainly, he says: 'These men revile'.

At first you are horrified, and then you are rather fascinated that they can take these tremendous truths of the Bible and simply revile them and show no reverence at all; and it begins to undermine your faith. And Jude says: Well, they are reviling things they don't understand at all. What do they understand? He's very rude here. He says that the things they understand are the things that animals understand; their instincts, their nature. And that explains their behaviour.

A lecturer in one of the London hospitals took a great deal of interest in the Christian students. He taught them Christian truth, he showed more interest in them, it seemed, than any of the churches around. He claimed to have real spiritual understanding and insight from God, he told them not to go to any of the churches nearby; he told them they would be misled if they did. He set himself up as the spiritual leader of all the really committed Christian students in that London hospital for a year or two. He spoke with irreverence of the nearby churches and teachers. He reviled the old ways. People were fascinated by his teaching.

The students in that hospital only woke up to the fact that they were being led far astray when he left his wife and ran off with another woman. It was then that they began to understand that he was a man of the flesh, not of the Spirit. But there were Christian students wounded there who never, so far as I know, recovered. Some came to their senses; others never did. The harm he did was very great.

You see, Jude is right up to date. He talks about things we know about. He's talking about people who seem to be very compelling, who seem to understand what is really going on, it seems that they understand the Word of God – but he says their understanding comes from another source.

Verse 11: Introductory

On we go then, to verse 11 and to those three characters, Cain, Balaam and Korah. I want to say first of all that I'm not going to follow the rabbinical expositions of these people. The Rabbis brought out expositions of Cain and Balaam and Korah in the synagogue, which were quite grotesque. I looked some of them up in the public library. By the time they had finished slandering these three Old Testament characters, all three had horns and hooves on and you could see the devil everywhere. But I want to tell you, that the people who represent these three in the churches today do not have horns and hooves. You don't recognise them.

Secondly, I want to say that I'm not going to go back and retell the Old Testament stories. It would take too long for the time we have together. So I'm going to assume you've done your homework.

Also, I'm going to look to the New Testament to control our understanding of the Old Testament stories. I think that's absolutely essential in all our Old Testament study, and in fact I'm going to look no further than Jude's letter to interpret the Old Testament picture and fill it out. Some of the much older commentators on Jude assume that after verse 11 he is simply filling out the three pictures; that Cain is represented by verses 12 and 13, that Balaam is represented in the next paragraph, focused in verse 16, and that Korah is represented by the next little paragraph, verses 17 and 19 – especially verse 19. I'm going to follow them and assume that there is a tie-up, and that all the way through the letter Jude is talking about the same people, the same characteristics or hallmarks. Each time, therefore, I'm going to start with a very brief summary of the Old Testament portrayal of these men, and then see what Jude has to say.

Cain

The Bible makes two things clear about Cain. First, *he was not a man of faith.* Hebrews 11:4, 'By faith Abel offered God a more acceptable sacrifice than Cain.' How was it that Abel was a true worshipper in this world? Because he was a man of faith. And how do we define faith? Look at Hebrews 11:1 and 3. Verse 3 in fact is a key thought in what I want to say this morning. You see, what the writer is saying is this: Here is this great and wonderful world around us, we can see and measure and investigate it all. But we can't discover the meaning of this world by anything we find *in* it. We have to go outside this world, to the wonderful Word of God on which it depends, before we can understand it.

It's very simple, not complicated; the man of this world looks within this world to explain it and its significance and meaning. But the man of faith, the man of God, looks outside it because he does not regard the world as self-explanatory.

That's a very simple distinction and a very important one. What we are told is that because Cain thought the world was self-explanatory, he did what the world always does when it comes to worship; he simply gave God what he had, he gave the best he could do. God would be satisfied with that, wouldn't He? – it was the best he could do. And that's the way of the world, the way of Cain. He wasn't a man of faith. It didn't occur to him that his way wouldn't be best.

Now turn to 1 John 3:11, 12, and the second thing we hear about Cain in the New Testament is that *he was not a man of love.* He didn't have the source, or the fruit, of real spiritual life within him. John very strikingly contrasts Cain with Christ, and in verse 16 he shows that the mark of Christ's love is that He laid down His life for other people. The mark of the man of this world is that he lays down other peoples' lives for the sake of himself. Christ is willing to serve others – the world wants to be served. Christ will sacrifice Himself for our good – Cain, and the world, sacrifice us for their good. A remarkable contrast which we've not time to pursue further.

We come back to Jude with these two thoughts in mind.

The way of Cain is, very simply, the way of the world. Cain is a man without true faith and without true love. He can't understand the ways of God, and therefore he can't understand the way of self-sacrifice. He is irritated by Abel, the man of faith, and in the end, as you know, murders him. Now, Jude says that many of these teachers who were infiltrating the churches of his day were men like Cain. They were men of the world, they were natural men. The great miracle of the new birth had never taken place in them.

With that in mind, I want you to look at verses 12 and 13 for some really vivid pictures of what happens when the churches receive ministers and leaders who are not spiritual men. These beautiful little pen pictures are, as always with Jude, progressive. One follows on from another and develops. As you follow them with me, remember; we are looking at the natural man in the assembly of the congregation of God's people.

First, *'These are blemishes on your love feasts ...'* The marginal reading 'reefs' is almost certainly the right translation, not 'blemishes'. They are hidden reefs in your love feasts, these men, in your agapēs, in your fellowship services round the Lord's table. Holidaying once in the south of France, we went on one of those little skidding boats you can hire, and we pushed out into the water at great speed. I was driving, I'm sorry to say (I ought to have known better, as a naval man ...). In those calm, beautiful, sunlit waters there were little hidden reefs. And we were going along at a great pace, four of us hanging on for dear life, and we hit one. Crunch! Down we went.

It's a very good picture, isn't it? Everybody's happy in this fellowship, the spiritual leaders who've joined them seem to be enjoying themselves (seem, indeed, to be enjoying themselves rather too much). Jude says, there are hidden reefs; it isn't until you hit them that they do the damage. You don't realise that they are doing the damage, they're hidden under the water. They are not true shepherds of the flock – they are looking after themselves! It's a very crude little picture in a way – yet all true to life. There is a certain worldly kind of minister who is very like that; and he is very popular at first . . . a hidden reef.

Now we go to the second picture which develops it a bit more. *'Waterless clouds carried along by winds . . .'* Let's go to the dry Middle East. There we are, parched with thirst, and the land all around us is dry and hard and cracked. We are longing for rain. The farmers are longing for it, the housewives, the young people, the older people – everybody is longing for a drop of rain. It's so dry! Then, one day, over the horizon comes a cloud – rather like Elijah's cloud – like a man's hand. And it builds up and spreads across the sky; and everybody rushes around, they can see what's going to happen. It's most exciting, it hasn't happened for months, and the cloud gets bigger and bigger and fills the whole sky. Everybody is waiting for the first drops to fall. They have come outside to feel the rain on their faces. And the cloud passes over the horizon and nothing falls.

Just so these new spiritual leaders are announced. You see, it's a dry spiritual time, and these leaders have apparently got a great reputation – they certainly say so themselves! And the church naturally expects that with this new man with his new degrees and so much being said about him, great things are going to happen. He's going to push out all the old ways, he's going to bring in new ways. He's full of modern alternatives and new things to do.

He comes to the church and he stays there for two or three years, and then – he goes on to a bigger charge. Everybody says 'What happened?' The answer is: 'Nothing happened. There wasn't any rain; no drops came. We are still as parched as when he arrived.'

Jude's next picture goes a little further. *'Fruitless trees in late autumn . . .'* I have a friend who is a fruit farmer. At the moment he is grubbing up a lot of his trees because they won't produce enough fruit at the right price. These men are rather like that; they haven't had enough fruit. They've been grubbed up.

It's exactly the same picture. These are brilliant men in the modern idiom. They've been put in a charge, and they spend two or three years there, they're always heard at Synod, they're always talking, they're always producing articles.

And it becomes clear after a year or two that on the local scene they are completely useless; and the leaders – the other elders, the deacons – come to the superintendent or the bishop or whoever it is and say, 'Would you please get rid of this man for us?' And the leader says 'What on earth shall I do? Oh, of course, there's that committee job ... We'll put him in Headquarters, he can drive a desk.'

And the next picture goes further still. Have you ever been in a real storm? Not unless you live on the Atlantic coast, if you live in Britain. But if you do live there you will know what a real storm can be, with winds reaching 140 miles an hour. I remember one in south-west Wales where the foam was carried by the storm for two nights, three miles over a headland into another bay. The foam and the muck was carried over the houses and was found for miles around. You see these men are beginning to be recognised for what they are. They are *'wild waves of the sea, casting up the foam of their own shame'*. Their particular way of behaving, their new morality, is beginning to show itself. It's covering the area where they live, it's having it's effect, it's touching other people. It begins to defile the church.

We go a little further. *'Wandering stars'* – possibly the planets, which were a puzzle because their apparently irregular movements. In those days the stargazers weren't doing it for fun or for the newspapers. They were looking at the stars to take their directions, and of course when these new people arrived, people looked to them for direction. What happened when they were led by them? It just took them into darkness. These progressive pictures are very vivid, aren't they? The Van Gogh colours really bring it right home to us. We've all met situations like this. I could name people and places where I've seen it happen. So I'm sure can you.

At first, they were like hidden reefs. No one could quite understand why these men were so apparently worldly. Everyone took it for granted that there was something there – but the clouds brought no rain, the trees no fruit. After they had been removed and put behind a desk where hopefully they could do no harm, the foam and the darkness became clear. They had led the people into the night, not into the light.

The tragedy of unconverted ministers – the disappointment and the heartbreak of the local church; the emptiness, the peril of these men when they are appointed to a church. There's nothing more to it than that. And yet, is that not a terrible situation for any church?

That's the first picture. It's a very simple one. The way of Cain: the way of the world.

Balaam

Now we look at the second picture, and I think there is a progression here. Balaam does not, as Cain does, stand simply for the man of the world who is irritated by the man of the Spirit and seeks to oppose him, as indeed wordly ministers and wordly leaders of denominations always will. Balaam is a different person, as you will know from your Old Testament, and I expect some of you will be thinking, 'Was he such a bad chap, after all?'

Let me tell you very briefly about Balaam. He was a brilliant young man with a great reputation. Even the king heard about him. Numbers 22:6 – what he blessed was blessed, what he cursed was cursed. God's hand was upon him, and God's Word was on his lips; and that was the man the king asked to curse Israel. What tremendous promise there was in the young Balaam! – promise that was spoiled and came to a bitter end, not only for Balaam but also for the people of Israel. Why was it, that this brilliant young man with this great spiritual gift became an enemy of God's people?

You know the reason. It says quite clearly here in Jude; he could not resist the royal blandishment, the riches and prestige of the king. Well, could you? You remember the contrast between Elisha, able completely to resist the gifts of Naaman, and Gehazi, who stood beside Elisha but was always dreaming of the profits that could be made from spiritual ministry. Now, Balaam is torn both ways. He doesn't seem able to make up his mind. He knows he cannot but speak the Word of God, and yet he wants to go in the direction of the king. He must have known in his heart that it was wrong. It was madness to play with it, and yet it was so appealing – and so flattering.

Finally the old donkey is the last to speak ... He goes back, you see, later on in his ministry, to see that godly woman who was his landlady when he was an unmarried assistant minister ... What a promising young speaker he had been then! The young had crowded into the church, they had brought their notebooks. They loved him. And the older people loved him too – what promise they had seen in his ministry! And now he has made a name for himself; he is travelling and moving in very important places – apparently he is making a great deal of money through his books. And he goes back to see his old landlady.

She's anxious; she asks him about the fame that has come to him, the new circles in which he is moving. With tears in her eyes she even – rather boldly – pleads with him not to lose what he once had. He's irritated with her and brushes her aside and when he gets back to his wife he says: 'She's an obstinate old mule, she can't see that what I'm doing is the only way forward for this denomination ...'

Maybe she did see. Maybe she did see the angel with the sword, which he never saw. But she was a humble soul, and she didn't matter in the world, and so he didn't listen to her. And his life became tragedy.

Now that is exactly what is being said in the next paragraph, verses 14 to 16. Look at verse 16 very carefully. I think it's a great pity if we just take these descriptions singly. This verse hangs together. *'Grumblers and malcontents'* – that speaks of a person who is discontented. Like the angels – you remember them, in our first study? Discontented with their supreme privilege of standing in the presence of God and ministering to the heirs of salvation. You see Balaam was discontented with that. Many a young person has been discontented with that. Brought into God's presence, given great spiritual gifts – but sent to an (apparently) unimportant place to minister to the elect. He seems to be in a backwater; nobody recognises him. He can't see why he can't break out, why the world can't see what he's got, and so he becomes a grumbler. That's a very deadly disease in spiritual workers. We often cannot understand why nobody has noticed our brilliant gifts and plucked us out into the limelight. But nobody has; and we grumble, and naturally, like all who are not daily ruled by the Spirit, *'follow our own passions'*. We are not to think of that in sexual terms – it's rather a bad translation here. He's just a man who follows his own worldly desires, who wants to have them tell him what could be his. What do you do in the world, if you want what it gives, if you want recognition? You *blow your own trumpet*; if you don't, you won't get far in the modern world. Unless you display your gifts, and tell everybody 'Look what I can do, look what I can say' – nobody it going to pay attention to you. Because today everything has to be advertised.

And what is the other thing to do if you want to advance in the world? Well, it says plainly here in verse 16, I must get alongside the people that matter, those who give promotion and move people around like pawns. It's so easy to look at this verse and not realise that it's happening all the time.

Take for example a young African pastor, he is wonderfully gifted by God. He is in a small charge, he is noticed by the missionaries, they take him off to Britain or the United States to study. My, what an impact he has! The complacent students wake up when this young African appears. He's not very well educated, but he certainly seems to know God; and people begin to ask, what is this secret? They are shamed into a new zeal for God. Here is a man who obviously knows our Lord Jesus Christ. He's like young Balaam. What he blesses is blessed, what he curses is cursed.

Then he gets back to Africa. He's now got a doctorate or whatever it may be. His relatives get around him; 'How can we possibly educate all our younger brothers and cousins on the pay you get as a pastor?' The powers that be begin to recognise him too; here's a man with ability, we mustn't leave him just doing this ... He begins to mix politics with the Bible. He makes a name for himself. He moves into the capital. He becomes an important person, he has the ear of

the government. Many years later enquiries are made,
perhaps by people back at that Bible college. 'What became
of so-and-so? What a shining light he was when he was here
as a young man!' Well, he's become a burden, a curse to the
church back in Africa.

*'They abandoned themselves for the sake of gain to
Balaam's error'* – and what started with so much promise
ended in such great tragedy, not just for the man but also for
the church.

Korah

Korah who perished, you remember, was responsible with
others for a rebellion against Moses. I'm sure that here, as
always with Jude, there is a progression. We can recognise
Cain; he is the man of the world, naturally hostile to spiritual
things. Balaam is the man with spiritual gifts who, because
he has not stood unequivocally for God, has turned against
Him. Korah takes us a step further.

I think Korah must have been an outstanding man. We are
told that when he fomented this rebellion 250 leaders,
chosen from the assembly, well-known amongst the people,
stood with him. Moses and Aaron were isolated. The leaders
were impressed with Korah. There was something in what he
was saying, yes, they would follow him. He said 'The Lord is
among *us*'; they said, 'Yes, the Lord is among *you*.'

Here is a man of apparent spiritual power and presence,
making great spiritual claims. Is this how Jude sees him?
Yes: look at verses 17 to 19. I want to explain verse 19
because it's not as simple as it looks. Most modern
commentators agree that the last two phrases describe the
nature of the divisions; that these men divided people, into
those who were 'men of the world, carnal', and those who
were 'men of the Spirit, Spirit-filled'. They went to the
assemblies, you see, and they made this division; 'These are
the carnal people; and *these* are the spiritual people – those
who follow us.'

Now with that in mind verse 18 comes alive. These men are
not like those in 2 Peter who scoff against the old truths –

these scoff against others; why, they scoff against the leadership God has appointed! They scoff against Moses and Aaron – 'Why should you be the only ones? We have been raised up as well!' It's possible that these people are more dangerous than the other two categories.

Now let me be very careful here. Please be very watchful as I say this. I am *not*, alas, saying that all church leaders are God-appointed men. I am *not* saying that all who protest against church leadership today are cynics seeking personal prominence. There are those who have not been appointed by God and there are those who rightly protest against them, in the power of the Spirit. What I *am* saying is that there is a true Christian leadership which we should recognise. And we need to be deeply suspicious of, and see the mark of Korah in, men who arise to divide congregations, who scoff at that leadership as obviously lacking gifts, who label those who follow it as worldly and carnal and blind to the leadership of the Spirit, who assume leadership themselves, who draw men after themselves, who set themselves up as those who would in that sense destroy the Body of Christ.

Conclusion

As far as I can see, all three categories are well in evidence today in the churches. God is doing new things amongst us, isn't He? Thank God for that. If the bad in our country is getting worse, the good is getting better. We see the churches coming back to life. We therefore see, all the more, the curse of Cain, the curse of Balaam, the curse of Korah. We shall not find that the devil changes his strategems. He never does. The things he does are the old tricks. We ought to be wise about them. He will seek to raise up unconverted ministers. He will seek out and destroy the gifts of promising young men. And we should watch him when he gets behind the Korahs – the Korahs are so impressive, but so divisive. What Jude says is very devastating. He says they divide people in this way: carnal and spiritual. But actually they are men of the world, they are devoid of the Spirit.

I want to try to summarise the men Jude mentions. I know

it's a long and complicated passage we've looked at.

Firstly, *these men are a great disappointment*. They are modern, they talk, they advertise themselves, there are many loud claims, but there is no lasting fruit to lay at Jesus' feet, and the mark of real Christian ministry is real Christian fruit. It is, to put it crudely, a matter of results. People turning from sin, people serving others, learning to love those who they do not love, churches staying together despite differences of opinion – that's the fruit of the Spirit. But these men, like Cain, are in the long run disappointing.

Secondly, *these men are divisive*. They are discontented, the spirit of the world has got into them and the spirit of the world is fundamentally discontented. It's always unsettled, it's always restless; it's always unwilling to submit to others, it's always sure and confident about its own gifts, it rushes in where angels would fear to tread, it has no hesitation about using worldly methods to advance spiritual ways. These men are divisive.

Thirdly, *these men are destructive*. They defile the flesh, they defile young people who follow their example, they deflect the church from its true path, they damage the churches and assemblies.

Now these are the three marks; but as you know, Jude puts it in one word. They are 'ungodly'. Verse 17: the apostles do not leave us unwarned. 'In the last times . . .' – Fear these men. Avoid them. Don't follow them.

3. The Impurity of the Church and the Individual Christian's Responsibility

You will remember Paul's exhortation to the churches, to speak the truth in love. It's an exhortation very much needed at all times, and Jude, following Paul, is a model of this.

I don't think you will disagree that he certainly speaks the truth, this brother Jude. He is warning the churches in unmistakable and unequivocal language. But he speaks the truth in love. Have you noticed that he writes to Christians as 'the beloved'? In verses 1,3,17 – and in verse 20, which is our starting point this morning; 'But you, beloved, build yourself up on your most holy faith.' He warns and wounds only to heal, so he begins with this word 'beloved'. We shouldn't think of Jude as a harsh and condemnatory writer. He is in fact (as you would expect of a servant of Jesus Christ) a man full of the love of God. He loves us as he writes and speaks to us in the name of God today.

Now in a sense, the main warning of this letter is over. It is summarised in verses 3,4. It is a warning to wake up, to look what is happening; because clearly he feels that many of the churches to which he is writing aren't really conscious of what is happening; they're complacent. I hope that none of us are complacent; what Jude has been talking about in this letter is the concern of every Christian. I very much doubt whether any of us are exempt from that concern; but the concern may be differently expressed in each case. If you belong to one of the main denominational churches, well, in

your church you may know what it is to face the
ministrations of people who've never been born again. But,
you may feel, you're safe from that because, maybe, you
belong to a house church. But are you sure that house
churches are completely safe from the ministrations of
people like Korah?

I don't think we can say that we stand apart from these
difficulties. No-one is outside the concern of the letter of
Jude. We cannot escape them, any more than we can ignore
them, until we get to heaven.

In a way Jude is a voice to the churches rather like those
politicians in Britain who in the thirties warned against
appeasement of Hitler. It's so easy – isn't it? – to slumber and
sleep, to feel we needn't arouse ourselves, it's not happening
yet. I had an aunt who was saying on 2 September 1939 that
'it couldn't happen'. There are many people in the churches
today who talk like that about false teaching. They say 'It
can't happen, you're not to get concerned; it's absurd to get
worked up.' There are many people, perhaps, who will be a
little sorry that we should have taken such a book as Jude
during our 1981 Keswick Convention. I hope not. Jude's
word is the Word of God and the Word of God is always a
word for today.

Now I say that Jude's main thrust is now over, because
recently one very fine commentator, in order to rescue these
words in verses 20 to 23 from just being regarded as
conventional language at the end of the letter, suggested that
they actually form its main message. I don't think we can say
that. But I certainly don't want to disregard these verses, as
though they were just devotional comments put in as
padding. They're not the main part of the letter, but they're
very practical and they're very necessary; and because I've
been so convinced of their practical necessity, I want to look
at them in detail.

Verse 3 and verse 20: The foundation

We come back at the beginning of verse 20 to 'the faith'. In
verse 3, we had to 'contend for the faith'. Now he says, you're

to 'build yourself up on your most holy faith'.

When he talks about the faith, Jude is not talking about your faith, or your trust, in your heart towards God. He's talking about the *content* of God's truth, in which you put your trust. It is objective, not subjective; and if you're a Bible student you will know that the later books of the New Testament are very concerned with objective truth. Paul, writing to Timothy and Titus, talks constantly of the 'sacred deposit', this truth that must be passed unharmed from generation to generation. Loyal men have got to be taught it so that they can teach other loyal men, who can teach other loyal men too. Obviously the apostles and church leaders towards the end of the New Testament era were concerned that this glorious gospel should not be in any way diminished or harmed by additions, and you get the same thing here in Jude.

He calls it 'the faith'. It's either 'the truth' or 'the faith' – the gospel. It's interesting that he calls it 'your most holy faith'. It's striking, isn't it? You would think that the only way you would use those words would be in referring to God Himself. To say that our faith is 'most holy' is significant; it is said, of course, because our faith speaks of God Himself. Christian knowledge of God does not come through mysticism. It doesn't come from 'looking within'. It doesn't come, either, from searching without; or from talking about experiences and comparing them. It comes through the truth, it is mediated to us through the faith; the faith that has to be known and understood. That's why doctrine is so important. I know it can be dry, I know it's sometimes put across in churches like a slab of rather cold meat. But actually doctrine is something of vital importance, isn't it? We come to know that most holy God through our most holy faith.

When I was young, I suppose most young people knew something about God, through Bible classes, Sunday schools and the like, in a way young people perhaps don't have the chance to today. And evangelists used to come to us saying: 'Well, you know all about God – but do you know Him?' And that was a very proper question. Now we need to change the question round today. We need to go to many young Christians – and many older Christians – and say, 'Yes, you know Him – but do you know much about Him?' You can't go on to know Him better, more deeply, in a way that is safe and sure, unless you know about Him. It's not enough just to say that Jesus is my Saviour. What Jesus are we talking about? It may be another Jesus that is going around in some churches, another gospel, another Spirit. The real Jesus, we know through our most holy faith. What a lovely phrase! It speaks of the source of the Christian faith, it comes from a holy God, and it speaks of the goal of the Christian faith. It leads to holiness.

That's very significant, isn't it? It is not possible to be sanctified without being scriptural; to grow towards holiness without a knowledge of God; to come to that goal without going back to that source; to have a most holy God and to come to love Him in a proper and Christian way without resting our faith and our lives on that most holy faith. Truth and life always tie up in Scripture, and they do here in brother Jude.

This then is the essential foundation on which these people are to build themselves up. One more word about it. Do you remember when it was that Jesus said He would build His Church?

All through those long chapters of Mark, Jesus is patiently leading His disciples to an understanding of who he is . All the time, He asks them that extraordinary question – 'Who do you think that I am? Who do people say that I am?' Wouldn't it be extraordinary if your new pastor at church spent his first three years saying 'Do you know who I am? It's very important!' It's all that Jesus talks about: 'Do you see what I'm doing, what I'm saying? Well then, who do you think that I am?'

Oh, how blind, and slow in understanding, they are; and then comes that wonderful day when Peter shouts it out. 'You're the Christ, of course!' And Jesus says: 'Now build My Church.'

The Church is built upon Christ, upon the faith about Christ, upon the truth of our Lord and Saviour Jesus Christ; and so our lives are built on the same foundation. Now that, of course, is why we fight for it, and I want to tie these two verses, 3 and 20, together very firmly in your mind.

Let me give you an illustration. From my office, I look out on two skyscraper office blocks. One is the National Westminster Bank building, forty-one storeys high (not a skyscraper by Manhattan standards!). Now imagine that security isn't as tight there as it actually is, and that I slip into the building before breakfast one morning, and I go down to the fourteenth basement and I take out my Boy Scout penknife; and I chip away at the wall until eventually I can take out a brick and throw it into a corner.

Now imagine I do that for several years, every morning of every weekday. Well, I'm no structural surveyor, but I would imagine that one day the surveyor would be making a routine report on the building and he'd find a great crack, perhaps by one of the windows. He'd want to say to himself, 'Well, it's just a decorator's problem.' But then he'd look again, and he'd make tests, and he'd get really worried. And before long he'd go down to the fourteenth basement.

Now you see that is exactly the situation in the churches of the West, at least in the churches of Britain, this century. Unknown to many good Christian people, there have been those who did not believe the 'most holy faith', who have found their way into the churches and have been taking away the foundation bricks of our faith – in generation after generation, church after church, denomination after denomination. And at Keswick and places like Keswick we've got up and said 'If you don't teach the first half of Paul's letters you won't be able to live the second half' – and many people go away and they say, 'Well, he's said it, of course, but we're still all right – perhaps we will survive, it seems that the building is still up, the Christian way of life is still happening among many people who don't even call themselves Christians; at least they are decent people ...'

And then suddenly, within a month or so, we look at our television set and we see a terrific crack by the window. What we've been saying is going to come to pass is coming to pass. And you can't deal with it by bringing in the decorators. You see lots of Christian 'decorators' around, with wonderful coloured paints. They'll come in; they'll slosh paint around; but you can't deal with it like that. You've got to go down to the fourteenth basement and you've got to put all the bricks back. And that's hard work.

Verses 20,21: Building on the foundation

Notice the extraordinary valuable balance between verses 3 and 20. We are to contend for the faith – battle for it – and we are to build ourselves up. Battle, build up: not one without the other. I suppose the tradition in which I've been brought up is very strong on building people up as Christians, it has a strong pastoral emphasis; and I thank God for that. But perhaps – as I've hinted earlier – I've rather taken for granted the battling side, I've left it to other people. It's really through the study of Jude (and, indeed, through other things) that I have come to see that every Christian is called not only to do the building up but also to do the battling. We've all got a part in it. And to go on doing the building up without battling for the truth is irresponsible; but sadly it is also possible to be taken up with battling for the truth and not to build oneself up.

I think we've all met people who have given their time and sometimes their lives to battling for the truth. We've come into touch with them and their friends, and maybe the societies they've formed; and we've been slightly shaken to find that they are often rather bitter and hard people. They are great controversialists but you couldn't say they are great saints. It's because we polarise. The battlers have not been building themselves up, and those who have been building themselves up have not been doing the battling. It's our responsibility to do both. After all, what is the point of being controversial and battling for the truth, if your life doesn't show anything worth fighting for?

But if we don't fight, there will be no foundation on which to build a church and a Christian life; and you can't build Christian living and you can't build a Christian minority in a society and you can't be salt and light in the world – unless you have a foundation on which to build. I want to put this

balance before you. It's a very important balance. We're
called to do both things. How then do we build ourselves up
in our most holy faith? Here Jude gives us three points (Jude,
as you know, is the patron saint of the three point talk).
There are three headings from a sermon here, aren't there? A
trinitarian sermon. Pray in the Holy Spirit . . . Keep yourself
in the love of God . . . Wait for the mercy of our Lord Jesus
Christ. What a splendid analysis of Christian living and
growth in sanctity!

Pray in the Spirit
Perhaps it is worth saying that this differs slightly from the
other two. My response here is not to the Spirit. In the other
commands I must respond to the Father and to the Son; but
in the first of them I am not told to pray to the Holy Spirit.
And this is because the Holy Spirit is wonderfully self-
effacing. He leads to the feet of Christ. When he has done
His work, the Church is praying, to God through Jesus
Christ. That's exactly like any Spirit-filled pastor or teacher,
of course. He takes people away from himself and fills them
with a spiritual capacity to draw near, not to himself but to
God.

Now we must have a cross-reference. Romans 8:15,16:
'You did not receive the spirit of slavery to fall back into fear'
– that's the mark of all non-Christian religions – 'but you
have received the spirit of sonship. When we cry, "Abba!
Father!" it is the Spirit Himself' – not itself – 'bearing witness
with our spirit that we are children of God . . .'

The witness of the Spirit is both an internal and an
external thing here. It is seen in an external result. 'We cry,
"Abba! Father!".' It's a children's cry, the cry of recognition,
of need, and of assurance: 'You belong to me and you have to
look after me.'

Some of the older Christians here will remember the book
Honest to God, one of the first heretical books to shake the
churches in this country. I was reading it in 1963, and I took
it as the subject for two Tuesday services among our
businessmen at St. Helen's. Unknown to me there was a
leading liberal theologian in the congregation, a woman

minister who was then very famous; and she gave me a thorough ticking-off after the service. 'Young man, you oughtn't to talk like that about such a distinguished scholar and his book. You don't know it well enough.' And she was a very distinguished scholar herself, with a very distinguished mind, but I'm sure God brought this to my mind at that moment: I said, 'I don't pretend to know all the answers, but did you realise that there is no mention in this book of God being a Father? And I don't see how one can call a book about God a Christian book if He's never a Father.' Her jaw dropped. She said, 'Well, Mr Lucas, I'd never noticed that.'

She was enough of a Christian woman to see that a book that talks like that is not a Christian book. Indeed in that same book John Robinson says that to him prayer is a problem, and that it is best seen in our human relationships, helping each other and so on. Well, yes, of course; without the Holy Spirit prayer is an impossibility, not a problem. But when the Holy Spirit comes the first thing He does is touch my lips and open my heart and give me a cry. Prayer is no longer a formal recitation; now it comes from the heart.

This is the first thing I must do to build myself up. Can anyone stop a Christian doing it?

The simple answer to that is that Satan will do all in his power to make you and me neglect this breath of life. If he doesn't do it to you I'm very surprised, because he can't destroy a praying church. And I thank God that when Satan gets after me (and he has sometimes given me cruel blows, he has knocked me down) – he knocks me to my knees. Were it not for his opposition and the temptations of the evil one, I think I would pray less. It's because I know that I'm up against the world, the flesh and the devil that I'm knocked onto my knees when I don't feel like praying. It must be very frustrating, I sometimes think, to be the devil. He has the bitter experience of attacking us and realising that every blow sends us back to prayer, and that's the thing of course which he hates the most.

Pray in the Holy Spirit. You won't pray without His strength.

Keep yourselves in the love of God

I've spoken already about the balance of Jude, and I want to mention it again. This word 'kept' is a great word of his. He began his letter with it in verse 1. It is the mark of the Christian that we are in the hands of God, and that He will not let us go and He keeps us. In verse 24 we read that we are kept for God. But it's interesting, isn't it, that though we are kept, Jude does not say 'I am kept by God, therefore my responsibility is to rejoice in His keeping power and simply trust Him – Lord, over to You: You keep; I trust.'

It's a conventional, pious response; some people do talk like that. But it's only partly a biblical one. If I don't trust that keeping power I am indeed a man without faith and without hope. But – I must also *keep myself* (verse 21). That's the biblical balance, the biblical grammar. Without it I fall foul of a pietistic Christianity which simply says that the Christian life is a matter of faith, full stop. This is so important that I hope older Christians will forgive me if I just do a little elementary biblical grammar for the sake of young Christians who haven't got their grammar straight. (Many people never learn their Christian grammar at all.)

Turn then to Philippians 2:12,13. Do you see in verse 13, that wonderful assurance that the whole of our salvation is God at work in us? It depends on Him. God is at work in you both to will and to work. Not only to work – but to will it. To give you the desire to turn your heart to incline you in His way. Well, you say; that's enough – that's a great secret of salvation, and I'll trust God to work in me.

But you see what Paul says in verse 12. The response to that is to work out your own salvation in fear and trembling. Quite a difficult verse, that, isn't it? It's not superficial. But I think you see the biblical grammar. God works, so you work. God keeps, so you keep. We wouldn't have thought of it in that way. 'Well, if God keeps me, surely that's enough' – no; God keeps, you keep.

Now, coming back to Jude, what is he saying? Is he saying 'Keep yourself', or 'Keep God loving you'?

'You know God is waiting to love you, but He can't love you unless you allow Him to . . .' – no, my dear friend, it's not saying that. It's not talking that kind of miserable nonsense. God loves me all the time, like the sun shining in its strength. God loves me because God is love, not because I am lovable. It's His nature to love, as it is the sun's nature to shine. God's love for me never stops. But my disobedience, my lack of keeping myself, can harm, hinder or stop my enjoyment of that love, just like these Lakeland clouds and mists at Keswick. I hate them, don't you? On a sunshiny day there's nothing in the whole world like Keswick; but how I hate it when the mists come down.

Surely this is a vivid illustration of what it is not to keep myself; and you know, we don't. I'm so slack. I want to tell you, I'm talking about myself in these things. I find it so hard to keep myself in the love of God. I'm so slack and complacent. I find myself a misery some mornings in the middle of my work, and I snap the head off my secretary (inwardly, not outwardly), and I'm wishing I didn't have all those letters to answer; and I say to myself, 'Dick, why are you such a misery?' And the answer isn't usually hard to find. It's that one hasn't been keeping oneself in the love of God.

What do I mean? For me (I'm speaking only for myself now), God has made it abundantly plain that I am to meet Him first thing in the day. He will take no excuse. Sometimes I've been busy preaching and I've just had to prepare first thing in the day and then I've found that I've not kept myself in the love of God. I say, 'Lord, you knew that I had thirty-five talks to give today' – and He doesn't answer, because He's told me this time and time again.

There are many ways in which we keep ourselves in God's love. I don't know which it is for you. But if God has laid down certain things that you know He wants from you – then keep them! Keep those regular habits of prayer, of giving, of obedience in your thought-life, whatever it may be. If you want to enjoy the sunshine, you must 'keep yourself'. A vital cross-reference – because I think it's probably the source of Jude's own teaching – is John 15:9-11. Surely this is the seed-bed from which Jude got his material. 'Abide in my love' – keep yourself in My love, is what that means. If you keep yourself in My commandments, you will keep yourself in My love. It's the same thing, you see. Verse 10: 'If you keep My commandments', you will keep yourself in My love – 'Just as I have kept My Father's commandments and abide in His love.' Verse 11: 'These things have I spoken to you that My joy may be in you and your joy may be full.'

Now isn't that clear, over against the antinomianism, the anti-Law teaching in some extreme evangelical circles? These people say to you, 'No, no, all we're called upon to do is to love Him.' But that's not what the Bible says. It says: He loves us, but we need His Law in order to keep ourselves in His love. It isn't enough just to say, 'I love the Lord with all my heart.' It doesn't guard me from sentimentalism, from delusions, from self-deception. If I love Him, I'll keep His commandments. Love and law go together. In other words, I'll be careful to do what pleases Him.

Don't you try to do what pleases those who love you? If it displeases your wife to have the piano played at two o'clock in the morning, presumably you don't do it. If you're a teenager and it displeases your mother to find the bathroom under three inches of water in the morning, you try not to do it. We try not to do the things that displease.

That's how we keep ourselves in the love of God. It's such an important secret of the Christian life, isn't it? That love is there all the time. I keep myself in it, I enjoy it, I throw away the clouds, the mist that comes down and suffocates me and makes me a misery. I throw them away by the disciplines – not the feelings – of keeping myself in that love, by looking to those commandments, checking up; 'Am I pleasing Him? Am I doing what He wants me to do?'

Wait for the mercy of our Lord Jesus Christ unto eternal life
This one is surprising, isn't it? Different from anything so far. Before we plunge into it – I wonder if you've noticed that Jesus is referred to with great respect, throughout the letter of Jude? We are sometimes a bit careless in talking about the Lord Jesus simply as 'Jesus' all the time. It's good sometimes to take the example and model of Jude. Look at verses 4,17,21,25; Jude and 2 Peter, those very late letters in the

New Testament, are the only places in the New Testament where this is invariably done. Surely it's because there was a danger of the Christians becoming over-familiar, talking in a rather slack, 'pally' way which sometimes fails to respect the lordship of Christ. He is our Lord Jesus Christ; Jesus Christ our Lord. •

Now, what do we do in regard to our Lord Jesus Christ? We wait for Him. I think it's a very important balance to keep: between what we have now in Christ and what we will have. You see if you look at this, it talks about mercy, it talks about eternal life, and it talks about Jesus. All these are things we experience now. We experience life now in Jesus Christ (John 17:3). Christ has come to us now by faith, through the Holy Spirit, so that now I have the mercy of God in Jesus Christ unto eternal life – and yet Jude says, I have to wait for the mercy of God in Jesus Christ unto eternal life. It is going to be mine, not only now, but then. I do not possess all that God has to give me of mercy, of eternal life or of Jesus Christ. I must still wait for a great deal. How easily this is forgotten! In order to ram it home, I want to give you another cross-reference, 1 Thessalonians 1:9,10.

I want you to look at these verses, and ask yourselves: Is this the way you talk about conversion at home in your church? I realise that they have overtones of the gospel coming to real paganism, and yet it seems to me that these verses do describe real conversions today. Delivered from wrath now, yes; but delivered from the wrath to come. And we wait for that coming, that great coming, when He finally brings mercy. It's a great comfort, isn't it? That mercy is still to come, as well as being experienced now. I shall still need it then, however far I've advanced in the Christian life.

But the very best reference of all to this in the New Testament is Romans 8, and without Romans 8, understood in terms of waiting, we go far astray. Verse 24 – the Christian life is a life of faith, it's a life of love, it's a life of hope; and it's the 'hope' that's so often forgotten. It's a life of expectancy, it's a life of waiting. 'In this hope we are saved.' What is he talking about in this chapter? – he's talking about suffering, and he's talking about our spiritual weakness, in verse 26.

And what the Apostle is saying is that we still live in a world of suffering and weakness and that this marks the Christian Church and our discipleship. The outsider looking in will often say, 'Where is your God?'

What is your answer? 'But you're so weak, you Christians!' continues the outsider. 'I expected you'd all be conquerors of evil. But I see many faults in you, you are very human here! Where is your God?'

And we have to say that His victory has not yet completely come. Let us be careful of those Christian super-apostles who are always talking about wholeness as though it is our natural right, of living almost without sin and failure, of healing as a new birthright of the Christian, of perfect knowledge – when Paul says we see through a glass darkly ... all these are phrases which properly belong to the return of Christ. We live between the now and then. The first coming of Christ was a hidden coming; He came to die. And His Church is a Church under the cross, marked by weakness, marked still by suffering, so there are tears and troubles in it, torment and division. 'Where is your God?'

We pray, we keep ourselves in the love of God, and we wait patiently for the mercy of our Lord Jesus Christ unto eternal life. There will be no doubt on that day what the church is.

Summary

Now, my dear friends, I want to summarise these three things because they are so important, they are so characteristic of Jude and very characteristic of the New Testament.

First (and this comes from my heart, not just from my notes), *these disciplines are costly.* There is no Christian holiness without tears. Prayer is a labour as well as a delight. I can watch tennis for an hour without difficulty. I can listen to a speaker at Keswick for an hour without difficulty. I can't pray for an hour without difficulty. Obedience; that's difficult. To keep oneself in God's love is costly. To wait, to endure when all the other Christians hardly seem to

understand what you go through – that's costly. To endure
perhaps when your partner has been taken away, when
there's been some great disappointment in your life, when
God hasn't seemed to treat you as He's treated other
Christians – that's costly.

Secondly, these *three disciplines call for energy.* And the
more I see of brother Jude, the more I think he was a man of
great energy. Get up and pray! Keep yourself, don't slack
back! Wait expectantly! He means, wait with endurance,
with steady persistence. 'I'm going on, despite . . .' that's New
Testament endurance. And then look at verse 20: 'Build
yourself up.' No clergy are mentioned in Jude, by the way.
He's not saying, 'You clergy, get out and build the church
up.' He's saying, 'You Christians, get out and build the
church up.' Supposing there isn't a pastor, supposing you've
got a Cain, or a Balaam or a Korah – you'll have to build
yourself up then, won't you? And your family. It calls for
energy.

Thirdly, *these disciplines of Christian living are the best
defence against error and bad teaching.* I thank God for the
young Christian students He is raising up, but there's no
safety merely in scholarship or intellectual answers. I ask
myself: Who will survive in a theological seminary where
there is destructive liberal teaching? And I answer the
question from Jude. The survivors are not the men or the
girls who are clever and know the answers. They are the men
or the girls who keep themselves in the love of God and pray
in the Spirit and wait for the coming of Jesus Christ.

What's the best defence against the immorality in our
society (and it's invading the church, isn't it)? Who will be the
survivors with all this filthy literature invading our minds
and our hearts? – well, there's only one answer to that. Those
who pray in the Holy Spirit, who keep themselves in the love
of God and wait for the mercy of our Lord Jesus Christ unto
eternal life. In other words: those who build themselves up.
Nobody else is going to survive.

Last of all, and this is the most important: *these disciplines
are to do with* – not 'discipline', not 'techniques', not 'being
religious'; but with *our relationship to God.* 'Pray in the

Spirit ... keep yourself in the love of God ... wait for our Lord Jesus Christ' – it's all beamed on Him. As I've looked out at the immemorial hills of Keswick I've been reminded of the first two verses of Psalm 90. People come to Keswick to escape, to have a holiday. We all need somewhere to escape. But the Psalmist says, 'Lord, Thou has been our dwelling place ...' I look at the immemorial hills, I look at this whole space-time world, and I realise that nowhere in all that wonderful creation can I find an escape, a home where I can be at peace. The saints have always come from outside the world. The world was not enough, they've gone outside it, to their eternal God as their eternal home.

So what have we been talking about? We've been talking about that. Praying in the Holy Spirit, keeping myself in the love of God, waiting for the coming of Jesus Christ. It's just another way of saying, in practical terms, making God our dwelling place. If you don't do those disciplines, you will not make the everlasting God your dwelling place as others have done in all generations.

4. The Impurity of the Church and the Keeping Power and Purposes of God

Two practical words by way of introduction. First about the battle for the Bible – if you like, the battle for truth. I think there is a danger of thinking we can win the battle for the Bible simply by writing books and arguing about the authority of the Bible. We do have to do that; but it has come home afresh to me that the battle for the Bible is best fought by expounding it – by drawing the sword and using it. Then it speaks for itself, and people are unable to deny that it is the very Word of God. It's been a great privilege to hear missionaries here saying to me, 'I don't know if you realise, but Jude speaks exactly to our situation here' – or there – thousands of miles apart! No human word can do that. It's not my wisdom. You see, our confidence is in the inspiration of Holy Scripture; that when we open it and expound it, when we study it with care, asking for the guidance and help of the Holy Spirit, then it does speak to our contemporary world, to the very situation in which we are.

Secondly, a word about the battle for purity. I want to remind you, especially if you are young (though frankly this battle for purity is one we who are older have just as much), that the way to battle is not, again, to battle with these particular sins all the time, or to study the Bible to see what it has to say about them; but to grow in grace and knowledge of God. The positive answer to the battle for the Bible is to use it; the positive answer to the battle for purity is to do what we were told to do in our last study – to build ourselves up.

Now let's go on to verses 22-25. I'm going to divide our study into two parts; Jude's *compassion*, and Jude's *confidence*. First,

Verses 22,23: Jude's compassion

I have to tell you that there is here that very rare thing in the New Testament – and I thank God that, in His providence, it is rare – an example of textual corruption. It is probably impossible now for the translators to discover with absolute certainty every word of the original of verses 22,23. That is why in a number of translations you have small differences. The main controversy is whether Jude is talking about three kinds of people, or two. If, like me, you think Jude is the patron saint of three-point talks, you will be likely to think it's three, and most of the modern translations assume this. The RSV does; and one of the best examples is the Good News Bible. The New English Bible, on the other hand, takes it as a twosome. I am not going to come down on one side or the other because I honestly don't know.

A number of words are slightly in question here, also; 'doubter' might be 'disputer'; but I can't say that's a great difference because most doubters are disputers, and vice versa. Too much can be made of all these differences. The message is quite clear. Indeed, it's what we would expect after verses 20 and 21. There we had the urgent words from Jude not to stand back, deploring these things and wringing our hands; not even to enter into controversy and think that that is enough; but also to build ourselves up on our most holy faith.

Now we would expect him to talk not only about our duty to ourselves, which is, to grow in grace and the knowledge of God; we would expect him to say what we should do for our believing friends who are caught up in this whirlpool and have been wounded by this false teaching and immorality.

And that's what he does in verses 22 and 23. He says, you have a duty to go after them in compassion and try to win them back. It's that same vigorous, wise, earnest call to counter the influence of the evil men. In this little letter I'm sure you've noticed this battle that is going on, between the destroying activity of Satan and the building activity of the Holy Spirit; and we are to side with the Holy Spirit and contend with Satan as he seeks to destroy the Church.

Actually, today you can see this happening in the Church a great deal. There are a great many spiritual vandals. I take one example – I can only speak for my own denomination – our training colleges in the Church of England. One can see the battle between destruction and construction going on; one can look at many of the liberal colleges in the last fifteen years and their record is a sorry one. The result has been destructive to people's faith and morals. On the other hand we can thank God for our evangelical colleges, that have sought through the preaching of the truth to be constructive, to send out men who are able to build the Church, not destroy it.

Jude's compassion should be a surprise to nobody, though it seems to be for some modern commentators. They can't make out how Jude can launch into the attack against these men and still show himself in the end to be a man full of mercy and pity. But I hope you can see that this is a true biblical balance, a balance of the Holy Spirit. God's mercy is mentioned a number of times in the letter; you will find it in verses 2 and 21. I want to remind you that the attributes of God are not static but dynamic. The Bible never, for example, simply admires the righteousness of God. It tells that if God is righteous He will be exercising wrath against evil and sin; He will be doing that now, because He is righteous; and He will be justifying those who believe now – because He is righteous. If God is merciful it means that God, in mercy, is constantly coming towards men. It's very important to say this, because if we are to be like God, feeling must be translated into action; the steam – to speak in terms of the old steam trains – must get into the pistons.

In many Christian meetings today, all you can hear is

steam and noise. If we're followers of Jude we've got to say that that steam has to get into the pistons, to drive us into Christian living, along the rails of Holy Spirit-guided living. What Jude is saying is: 'Look – if you really believe these things, if there really is mercy in your heart, then go out and convince the doubters; go out, and snatch them from the flames; go out even to the person who is stained by sin, and try to bring him back, in the power of the Spirit.'

I found I needed this particular word, when I studied Jude. It's so easy for Christians to be isolationist, to depend on the safety of our congregation and our friends; to feel that when people have gone into doubt and unbelief and immorality there's nothing we can do; almost to wash our hands of them, and feel 'Let's keep the Christians here safe, let's not go out into this perilous territory.' We fear rebuffs, we fear our inadequacy, we're shy. But that's wrong! What Jude is saying here is that we must not be content with the fellowship within; we must not treat the Church like an isolation hospital, fearing to step outside lest we catch a germ. If we have in our hearts the mercy and compassion and pity of God, we are bound to be driven out to bring them back. Are you thinking of somebody at this moment? You should be. In your heart, at this moment, pray for somebody you know who has been caught either by false teaching or immorality and has wandered from the Church. Ask that God will send either you or somebody else to bring them back.

I think this is a family matter, because brother James feels the same way. You remember how he finishes his letter – it's rather an untidy finish, you expect him to come to a very tidy conclusion but he tags on a kind of epilogue, 5:19. It's interesting that they've both got the same concern. James says: 'Remember; you've read my letter – but don't stop there, go out and bring back the wanderer.' It throws light on the household in which Jesus lived. And one of the great doctrines, which I think Jesus teaches in the Gospels, is to do what you can; and both James and Jude tell us to do that. So what does Jude's compassion lead to? It leads to action. Jude is always a man of action.

Now I try to answer the question, What does compassion *not* lead to?

Compassion does not lead to compromise with evil. I've said it before and I'll say it again; if we stand up and rebuke evil, people today will say that we lack pity, compassion and sympathy. That is not so, according to Jude. He is certainly compassionate, we know, and full of the mercy of God, but he warns us plainly about these men who are spoiling the Church. We may put it carefully, like this; Jude does not so much stand up and condemn these men – that's always dangerous, isn't it? Because we know our own hearts – he stands up and points to God's condemnation. He opens the Bible. He says: 'This is the God of the Bible – I warn you!' It's never wise to be personally scolding and condemning people. We're sinners too – we're not their judge. The Christian, surely, is called in compassion and truth simply to point to the Bible and therefore to the God of the Bible.

So I'm bound to tell you that the God of the Bible is a severe God when it comes to false pastors, shepherds, teaching and immorality. Look at verse 5. Look at verses 14, 15, where Jude quotes from Enoch (a book much loved in his generation). Jude does not stand up and condemn, though as a Christian leader in the early Church I suppose he had every right to do so; he points to God and says, 'I warn you: indeed, it is my compassion for you that makes me warn you.' The compassion that many speak of today is very cheap stuff. If you really have compassion in your heart you will tell people the truth.

There is a story about Dr Martyn Lloyd-Jones, possibly apocryphal, though I believe it to be true. After the War, he was asked by some ecumenical leaders to discuss their differences. They said that these differences really only concerned the Bible; if they could be resolved, everybody would be able to work together. So could they meet to discuss their view of the Bible and his view of the Bible? Apparently, Dr Lloyd-Jones agreed on condition that he could read them a paper.

They probably expected a paper on 'The authority of the Bible'; instead, he read them one on 'The God of the Bible'.

When Dr Lloyd-Jones had read his paper to them, one of the ecumenical leaders said to him, 'Well, of course we can't work together, because we're worshipping different Gods.'

I feel this is very important. Our difference is not so much over the Bible as over the God the Bible declares, it's as fundamental as that; a god who does not judge sin, the god of universalism, is not the God and Father of our Lord Jesus Christ.

In the end, as all Christians must say, there's only one answer to the question, 'What does God think?'; and that is, 'What did Jesus say?' He is that perfect way to the Father. What did Jesus say?

I can only tell you that the woes that Jesus spoke of make verse 11 of Jude pale into insignificance. Have you ever read Matthew 23? Read it now. Listen to the Lord Jesus Christ, the Son of God; the God who is love sent Him to save us, so we know perfectly well Jesus is full of compassion. These words were spoken by the compassionate Christ. They certainly make me tremble. They ought to make today's churches – certainly many of their leaders – tremble. Read Matthew 23:13 – isn't it true? Read verse 15. Read verse 25: 'Woe to you, scribes and Pharisees, [church leaders] hypocrites! For you cleanse the outside of the cup [you run beautiful services] . . . but inside they are full of extortion and rapacity . . .' Verse 27: 'Woe to you . . . you are like white-washed tombs, which outwardly appear beautiful, [clothed with the most beautiful vestments] but within . . . full of dead men's bones and all uncleanness.'

So now we know what compassion means. It means not shrinking from speaking the truth. Jude warns these evil pastors of what their way is leading to. And I want to speak a word of warning, through this talk, through the tape recordings and the Report, to all church leaders who are tampering with God's truth and with the standards of morality that Jesus laid down. They're not my words, I don't stand in judgement of you. But Jesus Christ most certainly does, and you are warned by His words. Our compassion wants to save you, not condemn you.

Jude also warns the *believers* of the power of evil. He

doesn't simply warn these false teachers, he comes to his brethren and he warns them, and you see this at the end of verse 23.

Verse 23: A balanced compassion

I find this balance very helpful. I find myself wanting to urge you to go out to these doubters and disputers. I think of a number of theological students I know who have been caught in these liberal colleges. I long to go out and win them back. They've got no ministry – it must be so miserable! I long to urge you to do the same; but I do realise the dangers; and I know some might say to me, 'Well, you know, we had somebody in our congregation who did this kind of work – and they got contaminated, they got snatched up in it.' So I'm very grateful that good, honest, practical Jude tells us at the end of verse 23 – and there's no doubt what he means – that when I go out in mercy, I'm to go out in fear. That is, the fear of God; 'hating even the garment spotted by the flesh'.

Isn't that helpful? I've got to go out to the sinner, but I've got to be very careful that in my heart there's a hatred for the sin that contaminated him. If I'm to do any good, I must sympathise with those who have been led astray; I must sit down with them, I must try to understand them – but that can so easily slip over a narrow boundary, can't it? – to begin talking sympathetically and understandingly about evil. I've got to go out to the leper – in a sense, like Jesus did, I've got to touch him – but I'm not Jesus, am I? I can't avoid being contaminated, unless by the power of the Spirit I hate sin.

How is it in your heart? Do you hate sin? I ask myself that question, because I love some darling sins very much, and I know that's wrong; and I ask the Holy Spirit to give me a new hatred of those sins. I'm so glad when God shows me – sometimes, I'm afraid, in another person rather than in myself – how ugly these things are, how miserable these sins make us, how sad they are.

I thank God when He shows me how these sins grieve His Holy Spirit; and I thank God when He reminds me that these sins pressed Jesus into the abyss of hell. I must hate sin as well as love those who've been drawn away. There must be within me this protection.

There is the balance. It's dangerous to say the one without the other, so I give them both to you, and I ask you to pray them in and make them practical in your own life and in your own church. We might summarise by saying that it is difficult and dangerous work, but we must also say that it's divine work, because any work of saving and rescuing is a work that is very close to the Saviour's heart.

Practical compassion – some examples

Now one or two words by way of application. First, *the abnormal rescuing*. Verse 23: '. . . by snatching them out of the fire'. As usual, of course, Jude's mind is saturated with Old Testament references, and he has two in mind. One is Amos 4:11, and the other one is Zechariah 3:2-4. Now isn't that interesting? The two scriptures which were saturating Jude's mind when he was talking about snatching people from the flames of impurity, have to do with rescue operations mounted by angels. Jude is full of this ministry of angels. And he makes the angels represent the most privileged servants of God, and by derivation they mean the privilege of the minister on earth. To do this angelic work is to share in the ministry of angels.

But I think I have to say, if this is the ministry of angels, it's the most difficult thing the angels ever had to do. What a thrill, to be chosen to be the one angel to be in the tomb to announce that Christ is risen! I guess there were a lot of angels queuing up for that one! But I guess there were no angels queuing up for Genesis 19. I can't imagine a more embarrassing and difficult work than the work they were sent to do in Sodom and Gomorrah. I mention this because Jude had it in mind. He was thinking of the practice of homosexuality. I feel that today we have to mention this, because it's in his mind in this letter, and it's in Genesis 19 – whatever some commentators may say. Read just a few verses from this extraordinarily vivid chapter; verse 4 – it's appalling, isn't it? The angels come down to Sodom, and this is the treatment they get. Verse 9 – poor Lot; he stands there, the compromised Christian, the compromised church, in the midst of evil – nobody's going to listen to him. What a terrible situation he's in!

When the angels see that the position is hopeless (verse 12 onwards), they say to Lot, 'Tell us who you've got here – have you got sons, daughters, sons-in-law? You've got to bring them all out of this place. The Lord is going to destroy it.'

So (verse 14), Lot goes to them and he says just what I've been saying today, the Lord is going to destroy: and, like the church so often does, they said 'You must be joking.' And poor Mrs Lot – she was thinking of those bridge parties, wasn't she, and those fashion shows. She just couldn't bear it, and (verse 26) she looked back and was caught up in the judgement.

What a picture of a church unwilling to accept the truth of the letter of Jude today; unwilling to believe that we're living in a society which is becoming like Sodom and Gomorrah, and unless the mercy of God is great upon us, we'll be destroyed; unwilling to believe the ministry of angels; unwilling to believe the warnings. It seems to them that we're just jesting. Yes, it's a very difficult work.

That's an abnormal situation, and in order to say something about the 'how' of compassion, I want to turn to *the normal way* in which we do it.

I speak now to all Christians, and especially leaders, Bible class teachers, ministers and pastors. Here is the normal way. You may not be up to that angelic ministry, but you can at least do this – it has been such a help to me in my ministry. We find it in 2 Timothy 2:22-26. The Lord's servant must not be quarrelsome, but be kind to everybody, an apt skilful teacher, just going on, teaching the truth, telling the sinner what the situation is; correcting him gently, because he's caught by the devil; and leaving it to God to release him in His own good time.

The same thing is said in chapter 4:2,3, and that verse has been another great blessing to me as I hope it will be to every minister here. Be unfailing in patience and teaching. You've just got to go on slogging away skilfully. Go on teaching, patiently do it, aptly do it; don't lose your temper, don't lose heart. Gently, patiently, forbearingly teach.

Verses 24,25: Jude's confidence

We must go on now to 'Jude's confidence'. Thank God for his confidence! He sent us out into the world to do this work, but he has confidence that despite its dangers we shall be kept, for he says this lovely doxology in honour of 'Him who is able to keep you from falling and to present you without blemish'.

Jude is in no doubt about the perseverance of the saints. One person came to me worried about verse 5 – surely God having saved would not destroy? But verse 5 speaks about churches. And when you see a church where faith and purity have gone, then that church has ceased to be a church. When you see a church where the poison of unbelief and impurity has got so deep into the bloodstream that the body can't eject it, then the hand of God's judgement is very near. But in those churches, God will still keep His people, and there will sometimes be times when those people have to be snatched out. But until that time comes, we must contend for the faith.

What the lovely miracle of verses 24 and 25 teaches me is this. Though this old world of ours gets more and more corrupt, and even if in our despair we see corruption encroaching on the churches, and even if we see the worst kind of sexual perversion coming, as it seems, into the Body of Christ – yet I am taught by these verses that I worship a God who is able to keep us from falling and to present to Himself on that great day a Bride who is perfect and faultless – that is miracle! He's going to do it!

Sometimes when I see all the filth that is around today, which wasn't around when I was a young Christian, I marvel at the way God keeps young Christians today. I see their shining faces, and I see them praying, and I see them winning their friends – and I thank God that I believe in a God who is able to keep them from falling. But it's a miracle, isn't it? It's not because they're stronger than other people; it's miracle. The great miracle of the last days – that out of all the corruption, when the judgement of God is falling upon a sinful world – there will emerge, coming down from heaven, a Bride that is perfect.

Now, let's look at the two striking words in verse 24. One of them is unique to the New Testament; and I want to be very exact here.

First, He is able to keep you from falling – the word comes from horse-riding, it's used of a sure-footed horse. You see these brilliant riders on television; they go over a fence, the fence comes down, and they manage to keep the horse from stumbling or falling. They go down steep hills, and because of the perfect control they have over the horse it goes down carefully, feeling its way, instead of slithering and sliding. That's the vivid Greek word used here. God is able to keep His people from falling, and they are calm and controlled and collected. Does your heart leap for joy when you hear that? It ought to. I thank God for the number of times, when I've come down at a fence, He's picked me up and got me going again. He keeps us from falling.

The second phrase in verse 24 uses a sacrificial word: He presents us without blemish before the presence of His glory. It's an Old Testament word, speaking of the perfect sacrifice, without any blemish whatsoever. It speaks of the future. The first phrase speaks of the present – He is able to keep me from falling now; the second looks to the future – He is able to keep me so that on that last day I shall be absolutely faultless. When He comes I shall be pure as He is pure – 1 John 3:2.

Now, my dear friends, I want to give you some more grammar. You must keep the present in the present and the future in the future. Don't put the future in the present! Don't teach that Christ makes His people faultless now. That is not true; those holiness movements in the Victorian era, and those holiness churches – some of which continue to this day – that teach that by the power of the Spirit I can be faultless now, are teaching something the Bible does not teach. Read 1 Thessalonians 5:23,24. 'He will do it . . .' – But He will not do it finally, until the coming of our Lord Jesus Christ. We must not wrest Scripture to our destruction. 'If we say we have no sin, we deceive ourselves, and the truth is not in us' (1 John 1:8).

We shall be faultless, without blemish, we shall be pure as
Jesus is pure – it's unbelievable, but we shall be, on that day.
The processes of sanctification are slow but sure. But don't
put the future into the present.

However – don't put the present into the future! He can
keep you from falling now – there's no need to put that into
the future! It's necessary that I should believe that. It's one of
the purposes of Keswick to raise our faith to believe that God
is able to do what He says He can do. I may be a poor old
horse, but He is a wonderful trainer. He is able to keep me
from stumbling, and to keep me going over this difficult
territory, calm and controlled.

It's important to realise that verse 24 is not just a
wonderful doxology; it's very accurate language, as always
in the Bible. 'He is able to present me . . . with exceeding joy.'
With wild, exultant joy! You see what Jude is doing? He
comes on the scene, he has every reason to be frightened,
there's a battle raging in the churches; and he tells the people
about the battle, and what they've got to do, that they've got
to get into training – but he says to them, never fear, the
battle is won. The God who called you and loves you and
keeps you is able to keep you to the end.

I am greatly moved when I read the story of Field-Marshal
Montgomery of Alamein, when he came up from Cairo to
take over the desert forces. He called all those disheartened
senior men together, and his Chief of Staff says that you
could have heard a pin drop in the sand of the desert. He told
them that Rommel was going to be defeated, that the battle
was over; and having issued his orders, he said 'You're not to
wake me!' and went to bed. In the night, his Chief of Staff
received urgent bad news, woke him, and got a terrific rocket
from Monty. It really is astonishing. Here is this almost
unknown general, arriving at the moment of greatest danger
in the history of the War; he tells them that defeat is over,
victory is certain, and he's so certain he refuses to be woken
up!

Now in the New Testament, there is something greater
than that. General Jude arrives on the scene, sees that the

Christians are in danger of defeat, warns them and puts them into training; he has no doubt, just as Monty had no doubt, about the necessity of training; but there's no panic whatsoever, for the God we serve is the God who is able to keep us from falling and, long before battle was ever joined, told us there was certain to be victory. That's a God worth having, isn't it?

So although we may have been alarmed during these studies, there's no need to panic. He's a great God. If He has begun a good work in you He will keep you. One day we, and many, many millions besides – a multitude without number – will be rejoicing with great joy.

In ten days from now, I shall be going down to a special place I know in Fleet Street (I'm not going to tell you where it is!), to watch the wedding procession of Prince Charles and Lady Diana. On that day, the whole city of London is going to go wild with rejoicing as the bride comes down to St Paul's Cathedral to marry her Prince Charming.

What Jude is talking about is something infinitely greater, which is beyond our imagination: when the Bride comes down from heaven to marry the King of kings. That's what Jude is talking about in verses 24 and 25, and that's where he very wisely lifts our hearts, lest we should panic. But of course we cannot stay up in the heavenlies; we've got to come down to earth when we leave Keswick. The enemy hasn't given up. The fight is on, and so we must go back to it.

Let us pray.
'Now to Him who is able to keep you from falling ...'

– you weren't believing that, were you? So we'd better start again. You don't really believe it yet, do you, in your heart? Do you believe it? Will you say it in your heart, with faith?

– Now unto Him who is able to keep you from falling, and to present us faultless, without blemish, before His presence with exceeding joy; unto Him be glory. Amen.

BY HIS GRACE, FOR HIS GLORY: PAUL'S LETTER TO THE EPHESIANS

by Rev Alan Flavelle

1. The Riches of Grace (Ephesians 1:1-2:10)

Three factors in the letter to the Ephesians give it a particular relevance to our day. First of all, it stresses the sovereignty of God in our salvation, and is thus a corrective to the experience-centred Christianity which is so prevalent. Secondly, it stresses the centrality of the Church in the purposes of God and thus offsets the chronic individualism which is so often a feature of evangelical life. Thirdly, it insists on the necessity for a life of holiness, and thus challenges the low standards and moral flabbiness with which so many Christian people seem to rest content.

Now, let me comment briefly at the outset of our study on three matters.

The writer
'Paul, an apostle ...' He is a divinely commissioned messenger. How fitting it is in a letter where he will unfold the purpose of God for the world and for the Church, that right at the outset he indicates his own place within that purpose. God had laid hold of him. It is that which gives him his authority as a teacher.

The readers
He writes 'to the saints who are at Ephesus and the faithful in Jesus Christ' (I follow the RSV margin here). The 'saints' are not top-class Christians, the spiritual elite of the Church.

They are rank-and-file church members. They are 'faithful' – they are full of faith. Because of that they are dependable in their calling. The two words, 'saints' and 'faithful', describe what they are and what they should be. Archbishop William Temple was clearly thinking of the former when he said, 'No-one is a believer who is not holy, and no-one is holy who is not a believer.'

Note their double environment. They were at Ephesus, with all its moral laxity and permissiveness; but they were also 'in Christ': as the root is in the soil and the branch is in the tree. So the church is in Christ, deriving its life and its sustenance from Him.

The purpose
And then the greeting of verse 2 sums up Paul's desire for them and his message to them: 'Grace to you and peace . . .' No two words are more important in this letter than 'grace' and 'peace'. Grace is the unmerited favour of God, the root from which our salvation flows. Peace is a relationship word: indicative of the total well-being that is ours when we are rightly related to the Lord, the fruit in which our salvation shows. Looked at in another way, grace governs the relationship between God and man; peace governs the relationship between man and man.

Now the letter divides itself neatly into two sections. Chapters 1-3, Christian doctrine; chapters 4-6, Christian duty. What God reveals to man determines what He requires of him. Paul, as always, writes in the conviction that what a man believes governs how he behaves.

In this first study and the next we shall be looking at the section on Christian doctrine, and you will notice that there is a distinctive theme unfolded in each of the first three chapters.

The will of God revealed (1:3-23)

Paul sets forth the riches of grace: what God bestows and how man receives. Verses 3-14 are really a song of praise – it was suggested to me that I might very well sing this section to you! I won't sing it, but I want you to grasp that it is indeed a song of praise. It is what Principal John Mackay called 'doctrine set to music'. It is truth that sings, doxology before theology; one thought crowds in upon another as the Apostle trumpets forth the mighty symphony of salvation.

He begins: What an abundant provision God has made for us! (verse 3). He has blessed us with all the things that are mediated to us in the ministry of the Holy Spirit, covering the whole range of our spiritual need. He has blessed us in Christ, for again and again the Apostle reminds us that all God gives us, He gives in Christ; all he does for us, He does in Christ. And He has blessed us in the heavenly places, the exalted realm to which Christ belongs and to which we are lifted up in Him. And all this from 'the God and Father of our Lord Jesus Christ', the God from whom all blessings flow, who is to be praised and worshipped for ever.

Note that Paul speaks of three great realities of the Christian life, three fundamental blessings of the gospel. ·

The election of grace (1:3,4)

'Election,' wrote John Calvin, 'is the foundation and first cause of all our blessings.' Now of course there is a problem here: how to reconcile the eternal election of God with the responsible decision of man. We cannot do it, but we know that the two are compatible within our experience. We know God laid hold of us: we know we responded to Him.

Now there can be no doubt about the purpose of election, and this is what Paul is concerned to emphasise (verse 4). He tells us four things.

God chose us that we should be holy. Holiness in God requires holiness in all who belong to Him, and we should never rest satisfied with anything less. The American Reinhold Niebuhr puts it like this: 'The worship of a perfectly holy God saves us from all premature satisfaction with ourselves.' *God chose us that we should be blameless*. The word used here is the word used in the Old Testament to describe the sacrificial animal that was without defect, the word that is used in Hebrews 9:14 of Him who offered

Himself without blemish to God. We are to offer ourselves in a similar way to God. *God chose us that we should be holy and blameless before Him.* Our life is to be morally impeccable not only in the sight of man but of God, in the eyes of Him who sees everything as it really is. Lastly – I take the marginal reading of the RSV here – '*He has chosen us that we might be holy and blameless before Him in love.*' He requires not a pharisaical holiness, stern and cold and forbidding, but a holiness radiant with the loveliness of grace, a holiness with a Christlike face, with a truly human touch.

Calvin comments: 'The very time of the election shows it to be free. For what could we have deserved, before the foundation of the world?'

That's the first of the blessings – the election of grace.

The adoption of sons (1:5,6)
'We are sons,' wrote theologian P T Forsyth, 'not by heredity but by adoption; not by right, but by redemption.' Regrettably, the RSV omits the word 'adoption', but it is without doubt the great reality of which the Apostle speaks here. Adoption is well defined in the Shorter Catechism compiled by the Westminster Divines: 'An act of God's free grace, whereby we are received into the number, and have a right to all the privileges, of the sons of God.' This, like all the other blessings of the gospel, is by His grace and for His glory. Nothing manifests the glory of God so much as the bestowal and acceptance of His salvation. It is 'to the praise of His glorious grace' that God has highly favoured us. The word Paul uses is the one the angel addressed to the virgin Mary: 'Hail, thou highly favoured one.'

We are highly favoured by God. He has made us one with Himself, and so as we sing and celebrate the reality of our adoption we can say:

So nigh, so very nigh to God I cannot nearer be;
For in the person of His Son, I am as near as He.

The redemption from sin (1:7,8)

Man's fundamental need is his need of God, and the one thing that stands in its way is his sin. So here, in describing what God has done to deal with that sin, Paul uses a picture-word taken from the slave market. He uses this great word 'redemption'. And we must always remember that redemption is not simply deliverance from bondage, but deliverance effected by the payment of a price. The emphasis is always on the costliness of the redemption.

Three things we are told about this: first of all, *it is redemption in Jesus Christ*, for Paul never tires of reminding us that all God does for us He does in Him. Then, *it is redemption through His blood*. Hebrews 9:32: let us never forget that every act of forgiveness has the blood of the Lord God upon it. 'All is of God,' says William Temple. 'The only thing of my own which I contribute to my redemption is the sin from which I require to be redeemed.' Thirdly, *it is according to the riches of His grace*. Paul rejoices to magnify the grace of God, and in doing that throughout this letter and particularly in this passage he reminds us that redemption is as complete as the ransom is costly.

Seeing and sharing God's purpose (1:9-14)

Paul speaks not only of what God bestows on us, but also of how we receive from God. In verses 9-14 he shows how we come to get a view of, and have a part in, God's final purpose for the world.

There are four steps. Firstly (verse 9) *He gives us to know the plan of God*. A mystery, in Scripture, is something which lies hidden until God makes it known. It becomes an open secret to those who receive God's revelation of Himself. God gives us 'all wisdom and insight' – the ability to see into the heart of things. He gives power to understand His purpose for the world, to see what He is about. He also gives us the ability to know what action to take in a given situation, in sharing that plan.

Now, what is God's plan of which the Apostle speaks? He tells us in verse 9 what His purpose is. Interestingly, when

Paul speaks of 'uniting', or more properly re-uniting, all things in Christ, he uses a word which denotes the total that was set at the top of a column of figures. It's a word also used of the summary that comes at the end of a lecture.

Everywhere we look today we see tension, chaos, disorder. Sometimes we might think it's all chaos, there's no pattern to history, no purpose. But Paul assures us that God is at work to restore the whole creation to find its true head in Christ. The one thing of which we can be sure is the plan of God. Despite all the winds that blow and the turbulence of our times, God's plan stands sure. Look how Paul speaks about it here. The great unchangeable thing still stands: 'His will' (verse 9), 'His purpose' (verse 9), 'His plan' (verse 10), are inexorably moving towards their goal, their summary. And we who are His share a place in that plan. Doesn't that thrill you? That, as verse 12 says, God has caught you up in it? 'To live for the praise of His glory' – is that your ambition?

Well now, He gives us to know the plan of God – but how do we get to know it? Verse 13: *we hear the Word of God*. His Word is supremely the good news of salvation. This is what the Church must proclaim, what the soul must believe. Karl Barth put it like this: 'At bottom, the Church is in the world only with a book in its hand. And if we're asked, "What have you to say?", we can only answer, "Here something has been said, and what is said we want to hear." ' Is that your desire? To tune in to what God has to say through His Word?

And the effect of this hearing is significant. Romans 10:17, 'Faith comes from what is heard, and what is heard comes by the preaching of Christ.'

So; we know the plan of God, we hear the Word of God – and as a result, *we trust the Son of God*. We put our faith in Christ. In verse 13 Paul, 'you also, who have heard the word of truth, the gospel of your salvation, have believed in Him.' It is by faith that we receive and rest on Him alone for salvation, as He is offered to us in the gospel. In Luther's words, 'It is by faith that we cast ourselves on Jesus Christ for life and death.' I trust we have all done that.

And then (verse 13 and 14), '*you were sealed with the promised Holy Spirit*.' A seal was primarily a mark of ownership, distinguishing the genuine from the spurious. The Holy Spirit is also what the RSV here describes as 'the guarantee of our inheritance' until we acquire it. The word used doesn't simply mean guarantee or pledge. It means a first instalment – a payment on account. Our experience of the Holy Spirit in the here-and-now is a foretaste of all that God has in mind and in store for us in His grace. Dr Martyn Lloyd-Jones comments: 'The seal assures me of my part in the inheritance and the earnest assures me of the inheritance itself.'

So the Apostle sings his song of praise. He feels he is tracing the course of a great river of blessing that flows down from the hills of grace and out to a sea of glory, quickening and enriching wherever it flows. So he tells us that all God does He does by His grace; and all that He does, He does for His glory.

From praise to prayer (1:15-23)

Turning to prayer in verses 15 and 16, Paul mentions the twin marks of authentic Christian experience: faith in Christ, and love for His people. A Christian is one in whose life Jesus is at the centre. And, speaking of the necessity of love for God's people, Dr Martyn Lloyd-Jones says: 'Whatever else I am, I would rather spend my time with the humblest Christian than with the greatest in the land who is not a Christian.' Do you love the Lord's people?

Paul's prayer in verse 17 is characteristic. He doesn't want his readers just to be acquainted with God. He wants them to have a first-hand, person-to-person knowledge of the reality that is God. Wherever the word 'glory' appears in Scripture, it means the reality of what God is, and that's what the Apostle wants the Church to know; that's the burden of his prayer.

But more specifically he goes on to pray that they might have the fullest possible knowledge of three things. First, *the hope of His call*. Christian hope is grounded on what we know of God in His Word. It is the inward certainty that we have been effectually called, that the God-given inheritance is really ours.

It is a good thing for us Christians to think often of where we are going and what we are going to. And Paul next prays that we may be aware of the wealth of His inheritance. It is a similar thought to Romans 8:17; 'We are heirs of God and fellow-heirs with Christ.' The word 'inheritance' reminds us that all we need is already vested for us in Christ. But Paul recognises that it's not enough that we should have it, he also wants us to know that we have it, and be encouraged to possess it.

It is a great stimulus for us to know that we have an inheritance that is imperishable, undefiled and unfading, kept in heaven for us who by God's power are being kept for salvation. And he prays that they may know the greatness of His power, 'what is the immeasurable greatness of His power in us who believe.' Now I could spend all my time in this study talking about what the Apostle says about the power of God. Let me simply list the six things that he underlines in this short passage.

It is *power with vast resources*, 'power unlimited', as the New English Bible renders it. It is *power already at work in us*, for our salvation is a demonstration of what that power has already achieved. It is the *power that God exerted in Christ* when He raised Him from the dead and made Him sit at His right hand in the heavenly places, far above all rule and authority and power and dominion, and above every name that is named, not only in this world but also in the world that is to come. It is *power irresistible in its force and inexhaustible in its supply*. It is *power that gives Christ His authority* in our world and in His Church, for 'God has put all things under His feet and has made Him the head over all things for the Church.' Lastly, it is *power that the Church 'which is His body' needs* for proper functioning.

Now as the Apostle thinks about it, he is lost in wonder, love and praise. And as you and I try to follow him as he speaks of this power, that goes beyond both our apprehension and our experience, what better can we do, than fall prostrate before our Lord, and cry 'Thine O Lord is the kingdom, and the power, and the glory, for ever.'

The work of God achieved (2:1-10)

Now we turn briefly to the first half of the second chapter. Paul has shown that the purpose of God is to re-unite all things in Christ. He has spoken of the power that is available to carry through that mighty purpose.

But we cannot but be aware of the seemingly intractable problem that faces us in our world. 'The universe', said John Mackay, 'is rifted. History and the heart of man are rifted.' How then can God tackle the tensions and conflicts of our divided world?

In the first ten verses, Paul speaks of what God does to heal the vertical rift between God and man. And then, as we shall see in our next study, in the second section of the chapter he speaks of what God has done to heal the horizontal rift between Jew and Gentile, between man and man.

But in the first part of the chapter the Apostle not only shows the human problem, but also states the divine solution. The significant transitional phrase is at the beginning of verse 4: 'But God ...' God breaks into a situation, takes the initiative; He intervenes savingly. In verses 1-3, the Apostle outlines the plight of man. Time allows us only a mere outline of this searching diagnosis of man's state. Reminding the Ephesians of what they were before grace saved them, he sets out in these verses the story of their shame; and in so doing, he shows us ourselves. He demonstrates the power of God for salvation by showing what God has found in us, what He has done for us, and what He has made of us.

What God has found in us (2:1-3)
Man by nature is dead in sin (verse 1). He is dead to God and the spiritual world, dead because of his sins. He is dragged along by the world like a dead carcass (verse 2), pressurised by the godless world, relentlessly squeezed into its mould. The world by its glamour fascinates man and dominates him by its power, and thus drags him away from Christ; and he is duped by the devil – 'following the prince of the power of the

air'. Left to himself in his natural state, man is not only mesmerised but tyrannised by the arch-deceiver who embraces the whole world. As the result, men are smothered by the spirit of disobedience (which is the literal meaning of the semitic phrase Paul uses). It is man's nature to rebel, to defy God and go his own way.

Man is also dogged by passion. Paul changes from the 'you' of verses 1,2 to the 'we' of verse 3, to show that it is not just the pagan world that is morally dead and debased. People like himself, cradled in religion, suffer the same dread malaise.

Well now, there's much more we could say about this, but that is the outline of the human problem – a problem, according to Thomas Chalmers, 'fit for a God'. How amazing that Paul can follow it with his dramatic 'But God . . .'! God has done something about man's situation, and in verses 4-10 he outlines the plan of God.

What God has done for us (2:4-10)

May I finish by calling your attention to four basic things about our God-given salvation:

It is *salvation by grace*. 'Grace,' said James Denny, 'is the love of God; spontaneous, unearned, beautiful, at work in Jesus Christ for the salvation of sinners.' 'It is the gift of Christ,' said Karl Barth, 'who exposes the gulf between God and man, and by exposing it, bridges it.' Paul uses a variety of words here – mercy, love, grace, kindness – but the emphasis is the same: salvation is of the Lord.

And then, of course, it is *salvation in Christ*. Every spiritual blessing is ours in Him; it is therefore obvious that the most fundamental blessing of all is ours in Christ. Paul makes his point in five different ways, in verses 5-7. Here in all its fullness is the blessed truth of the union of the believer with Christ. Quickened in Him, raised in Him, exalted in Him, created anew in Him; we have been made one with our Lord.

And it is *salvation through faith*. On man's side, the union with Christ is effected through faith. Not only does Paul assert this positively, but he goes on to add a strong negative:

'This is not your own doing, but it is the gift of God.' A W Tozer makes a helpful comment: 'Faith is the least self-regarding of the virtues ... it is occupied with the object upon which it rests and it pays no attention to itself.' Faith – focussed on Christ.

And finally it is *salvation unto good works* (verse 10). Literally, 'We are His poem, His work of art.' A Christian is one in whom God has been at work. When the reformers stressed the phrase, 'by faith alone', they did not intend to play down the value of good works. Paul says here, 'We are ... created in Christ Jesus for good works'. We are not twisting it too much when we say, 'We as Christians are God's masterpieces.' He wants to hold us up before the watching world as an example of what His grace can accomplish. Could anybody point to me, and say 'There is a fine example of Christ's work!'? Is that your desire? That Christ might use your life as a 'demonstration model' – as a representation, to the world, of the kind of lives He can produce?

2. The Mystery of the Gospel (Ephesians 2:11 – 3:21)

The world of the first century was, like our own, a deeply divided one. Undoubtedly, the most deeply-seated division was that between Jew and Gentile. They were poles apart. Now, we have seen how in chapter 2 Paul rejoices to proclaim a message that was addressed to that situation – a message of reconciliation. He points to the Christ who breaks down the barriers that divide, and builds up the bridges that unite. It is therefore a message singularly relevant to our strife-torn and tormented society today. Having shown in the first ten verses of chapter 2 what has been done in Christ to heal the vertical rift between God and man, he now in verses 11-22 addresses himself to the other side of the question; and we start our study with this section.

The old hostility (2:11-15)

Just as today the West is separated from the East by what we call 'the iron curtain', and just as the white races are held separate from the coloured races by what we call 'the colour bar', so in the first century the Jew was separated from the Gentile by what Paul calls, in verse 14, 'the dividing wall of hostility'. But Paul shows in a fascinating way how God, dealing with the basic problem of man's relationship with God, makes possible a new relationship between Jew and Gentile, between man and man.

The deprived Gentiles

In verses 11-15, the first thing Paul shows us is that the Gentiles were a deprived people. Two words in verse 13 crystallise it: they were 'afar off'. William Hendricksen sums up their condition in five words: they were 'Christless, stateless, friendless, hopeless, godless'.

'You were at that time,' says Paul, referring to the time before their conversion, '*separated from Christ*'. And, as John Calvin says, 'So long as we are without Christ and separated from Him, nothing which He did for the salvation of the world is of the least benefit to us.' If all spiritual blessings are in Christ, then to be cut off from Him is to be unspeakably poor. They were Christless.

And, Paul says, they were '*alienated from the commonwealth of Israel*'. God's favour to His people was shown in a covenant. In saving them God formed them into a community of faith, set apart for Himself. The Gentiles didn't belong. They were stateless.

They were '*strangers to the covenant of promise*' – they knew nothing of the special relationship to God of which the covenant was the seal and the pledge. They were friendless.

And, Paul says, they were '*without hope*'. Fear and despair reigned over the pagan world as it does today. They had no assurance of the future because they had no knowledge of God. They were hopeless.

And –'*without God in the world*' – not knowing God. William Hendricksen: 'They resembled mariners without compass and guide. They were adrift in a rudderless ship on a starless night on a tempestuous sea, far away from the harbour.' They were godless.

'Therefore remember', says the Apostle, 'remember what you were before Christ changed everything for you.' And all of us do well to remember to do just that. Whether we think of the neo-paganism of Britain or the paganism of the wider world, it should stir our hearts profoundly to realise what it means to be without God and without hope in the world. The Gentiles were a deprived people.

The despised Gentiles

In verse 11 Paul makes it clear that there was a certain amount of name-calling between Jew and Gentile. There were two things which lay behind the superior attitude adopted by the Jew. First of all there was prejudice, which, as Dr Martyn Lloyd-Jones has said, 'turns differences into barriers'. The difference between Jew and Gentile, as we know, was due to the fact that God had called the Jew to a special role; and this tended to engender pride on his part. For just as cultured Greeks despised all other men as barbarians, so religious Jews despised all others as pagans. Jews could allege, for instance, that God created Gentiles in order to fuel the flames of hell. It's not easy for us to take in the fact that no strict Jew would assist a Gentile mother in childbirth, lest he be involved in bringing another Gentile into the world. Thus a natural division became a wall of hostility.

But not only was it due to pride, it was also due to the false scale of values that the Jew had. He boasted of his circumcision – a mere physical sign, said Paul; something made with hands. How often divisions in our world are due to purely external, peripheral things! The Jew, instead of acting in love to share with his Gentile neighbour the truth he enjoyed, came to despise him. Is this saying something to us, in the pluralistic society of today? We emphasise our traditions, our customs and standards; we express them in our slogans and our watchwords, allowing them to breed a spirit of enmity, forgetting that such things are of little consequence in the eyes of Him with whom we have to do.

Now, if I may say this to you; I am very conscious that we in Ulster – even with all our evangelical traditions – have erected man-made barriers which keep people at a distance, out of reach of the witness that we have been called to bear. Even as evangelical Christians, it is possible to ignore – or even, in our hearts, despise – those whom we call 'people of the other sort'. Shame on us, if we share the sin of the Jews who – custodians of the Law as they were – failed the Gentiles until everything was changed for both Jew and Gentile in Jesus Christ.

But God did change things.'But now –' says Paul in verse 13 (and that matches the 'But now –' of verse 4), 'in Christ Jesus you who were once far off have been brought near in the blood of Christ.' Sin was the great barrier, but Christ by His death has broken that barrier down. No one need now be shut out, 'for He is our peace who has made us both one, and has broken down the dividing wall of hostility, by abolishing in His flesh the law of commandments and ordinances.' Jesus made it possible for both Jew and Gentile to come to the same God, on the same terms, with the same rights. Thus the whole underlying cause of the hostility was removed. As one modern commentator puts it: 'The material for our divisions can only be melted down in the crucible of the cross.' And that's a lesson which we need, increasingly, to learn.

The new humanity (2:15-22)

God's purpose is stated in verses 15 and 16. The creation of the new humanity brings to an end the old hostility. Significantly, in verse 15, the Greek word 'new' means a new kind of thing which didn't exist before. God's way of making peace is to bring into being something entirely new; something which hadn't existed previously; namely, the Christian Church. Thus God's solution to the problem of our divisions is a radical one, dealing with the root cause of the trouble, our alienation from God. It is not that the Gentiles were raised to the status of Jews, but that both were given a new status, and on its basis, a new spirit of oneness in Christ. This is why, as Paul says, Christ 'came and preached peace to you who were far off' – the Gentiles – 'and peace to those who were near' – the Jews.

Why is it that Christ can preach peace? Why is harmony made possible in Christ? Because, says Paul in verse 18, 'through Him we both have access in one Spirit to the Father.' Have you ever noticed that our concept of prayer involves the whole doctrine of the Trinity? We need the Father when we pray, for who knows us and loves us and meets our needs, but He? We need the Son when we pray, for

He is the door into the Father's presence, and no other can give us access. And we need the Spirit when we pray, for only He can open our eyes to the reality of God and induce in us a sense of need, assure us of the promises, and direct our petitions. Do we genuinely rejoice in the privilege of prayer, in being able to come into the audience chamber of the King of kings? Do we grasp the privilege? Do we exercise this ministry? Or do we sometimes live, in effect, as if the door of God's presence were barred against us?

Unimpeded entrance into God's presence is not the only right given to Jew and Gentile. Both, alike, are now made full members of the Church. Verse 19: 'strangers and sojourners' are those who find themselves among a people not their own; but citizens of one kingdom, members of one family, should feel very much at home. They are in the kingdom not on a passport but on a birth certificate. They have a full right to be there. Do you always feel completely at home in your church fellowship? And let me ask you this – do you make an effort to make people of different age groups, racial backgrounds and personal lifestyles feel that they belong within the family?

I know some of the students will have read Os Guiness's book, *The Dust of Death*. He says, of the first Christians, 'they were a healing community, they were one in Christ, they were a Third Race. All classification by nation, race, ideology, religion or class structure denoted a previous reality now transcended.' Would to God that the Christian Church today exemplified that ideal!

Now what helped the Christians at Ephesus to demonstrate this oneness was the recognition of who they were and of what Christ had done for them. Paul says, you are 'built upon the foundation of apostles and prophets,' and they were the first members, the first stones in the building, 'Christ Himself being the cornerstone ... in whom the whole structure is joined together and grows into a holy temple in the Lord.' Still in the course of construction; let us never forget that.

And what was God's purpose in making His people 'a holy temple in the Lord ... for a dwelling place of God in the

Spirit'? In effect, Paul is reminding both Jew and Gentile that God's dwelling place is no longer a physical building but a temple composed of men and women who have been united to Jesus Christ. That's the Church. As he puts it in 1 Corinthians 3:16: 'Do you not know that you are God's temple and that God's Spirit dwells within you?'

Here then is a gospel for society. Good news for a divided world! We all come with the same need, we all come with the same faith, we all come through the same Christ, to the same God. That's why the Church is one.

The Word of God proclaimed

The theme of the third chapter is, the Word of God proclaimed. The Apostle writes of his own involvement in what God has done and is doing. Notice how he begins (3:1). He hears, as it were, the clink of his chains, and remembers where he is and why. He is in bonds because he has stood uncompromisingly for the equality of Jew and Gentile within the Church of Christ. (If I may interject this comment: you will find that a preacher is sometimes opposed not for faithfully proclaiming the gospel but for courageously attempting to apply that gospel to every issue that arises in society. And that was why Paul was in prison.)

The phrase, 'for this reason', shows a close connection between what follows and what preceded. Both what we preach and how we pray are determined by what God had revealed of His will and what He has achieved in His work. Paul begins to pray, but suddenly the whole thought of what God has done for him and the world takes hold of his heart, and so first, in verses 2 to 13, he tells us why he preaches. 'Grace' (verse 2) in this connection denotes the privilege of being given a work to do for God. Paul never ceased to wonder at the fact that God had entrusted the gospel to him.

At a time of great discouragement, Dr William Sangster nevertheless noted in his diary, 'But I am happy fulfilling my ministry. Born to do this. Marvelling at the goodness of God in allowing me to do it. Envying no man his job.'

Ministers and Christian leaders – do you sense anything of that in your ministry?

The mystery that has been shown to him (verses 2-6)
A 'mystery' in Scripture (as we have seen) is something that stays concealed until God chooses to reveal it. Knowledge of God and of His will come not by human discovery, but by divine disclosure. God in His grace enabled the Apostle both to perceive and to proclaim the message. Now of course some of the Old Testament writers knew that the Gentile world would share in future blessing. You find that for example in Psalm 72 and in Isaiah 11. What then does verse 5 mean?

The answer, it seems to me, is twofold. Before Christ, it was not made known ... 'as it has now been revealed'. Old Testament members of the Church had fore-gleams of it; but it was only to the New Testament apostles and prophets that it was fully revealed by the Spirit. Not only so; but the Old Testament saints did not see that with the coming of the Messiah the Gentiles would not be incorporated into Israel, but that a new organism would emerge in which Jew and Gentile would be one. In God's house there are no boarders – all are children of the one father. So the oneness of Jew and Gentile within the Church is stressed here when Paul says, 'You are fellow-heirs.' You are fellow-members. You are fellow-sharers in the promise, through Jesus Christ. That was the conviction that gripped the heart of the Apostle, and made him a flaming preacher of the gospel. And so he writes to us of,

The ministry that had been entrusted to him (3:7-13)
Mark this; Paul did not make himself a minister. It was not thrust upon him by the Church. Note his words: 'gift', 'grace', 'given'. Indeed, he takes a very low view of himself (verse 8). He coins a new word; the comparative of a superlative – 'I am the "leastest" of all saints.' God cannot fully bless the ministry of a man who has not been crucified and emptied of every degree of self-importance and self-display.

More than a hundred years ago D L Moody was at the height of his influence here in Britain. F B Meyer said of him, 'Moody is a man who seems never to have heard of himself.' How different it so often is in the Christian world! May God deliver us from self-centred attitudes.

What then can make one a self-forgetting Christian? Paul tells us: 'the working of His power'. Nothing less can do it. In Colossians 1:29, the Apostle shows how his whole ministry depends upon this power of God. 'For this I toil, striving with all the energy which He mightily inspires within me.' And what a ministry it was! 'To preach to the Gentiles the unsearchable riches of Christ' (Ephesians 3:8). Unsearchable riches – ocean depths that can never be plumbed, treasure stores that can never be exhausted. Enough for you and me and everyone, for ever. That's what we're called to minister.

What was Paul's aim in preaching? 'To make all men see'. To throw light upon the things about which so many are in the dark. To give them some inkling of the all-embracing purpose of God. Paul saw (3:9-11) that God was working to a plan, that he himself was an agent of that plan; and it was his great ministry and passion to share some understanding of that, so that other people might get caught up in it and might be part of what God was doing in a wonderful way in His world.

Are you part of that plan? To know ourselves part of it is to be freed from all fear, so 'we have boldness and confidence of access through our faith in Him.'

Let me say a little about that word, 'boldness'. It comes from two Greek words, meaning 'telling' and 'all'. It conjures up for me the picture of a little child, terribly troubled and upset, bottling it all up inside himself. And then suddenly he sees his father or mother and rushes up with outstretched arms and embraces his parent, and unburdens his heart, telling everything. That's what prayer is meant to be – telling God everything as you feel it. And that's a great antidote to fear, isn't it?

And not only does it save us from fear, it saves us from faintheartedness. So Paul can add verse 13 as a personal note. We need never pity ourselves or despair of our fellow-

believers when things go wrong or when suffering comes, or
when our fond hopes miscarry. So the Apostle is not making
light of his hardships but realistically assessing them, when
he writes in Philippians 1:12 that 'what has happened to me'
– the chains, dungeon and hardship included – 'has really
served to advance the gospel.'

Paul at prayer (3:14-21)

Because of what he had just written about the Church, he
recognises the need to pray that it might be worthy of its
calling (3:14,15).

If I were to ask you this morning what you would like to
see happening in the Church in this land, what would you
say? What are the missing things that you would like to see
present? Well now, keep that thought in your mind as we
finish our study, noting the four things for which Paul prays.
First,

The enabling power of the Spirit

Need I remind you that our basic need is the need for power?
Power to be what we are, what we have been called to be.
Paul indicates four aspects of this power.

It is *power according to the riches of His glory* – not
merely out of His treasures, but according to His treasures.
He gives without limit, because His grace is without limit.
And then, it is *power from God*, 'that He may grant you to be
strengthened with might'. You remember the words of
Psalm 62:11: '. . . power belongs to God'. Then, of course, it
is *power through the Spirit*, 'strengthened with might by His
Spirit', reminding us of the promise given to the early
Church in Acts 1:8, 'You shall receive power . . .' Now this
power is available to us, it is something God has covenanted
to us. Yet isn't it a tragedy that, as the great missionary
pioneer Hudson Taylor put it, 'we serve God to the limit of
our own incompetence, rather than to the limit of His
omnipotence.'? Fourthly, it is *power in the inner man*, in our
inmost being as contrasted to our bodies. It is the hidden
man of the heart which has been made alive together in

Christ. Paul prays that power may come into the inner life, to direct the mind, reinforce the will, guard the secret springs, the motives that control, to save us from our unpredictable moods, to make us whole inside. Power!

Then he prays, in verse 17, for,

The abiding presence of Christ

It is only as we by power are made mighty that Christ can dwell in us. The word rendered 'dwell in your hearts' means to 'settle down and be at home in your hearts'. It carries the thought of permanent residence. For us to know Christ, present in, presiding over the very seat of the personality, becomes possible through faith.

I keep on my desk at home a little prayer; some of you will know it:

> Lord Jesus, make Thyself to me
> A living, bright reality;
> More present to faith's vision keen,
> Than any outward object seem;
> More nigh, more intimately nigh
> Than even the closest earthly tie.

Are you making Christ at home in your heart? Are you seeing to it that there is nothing there that offends Him or dishonours Him?

And then he prays for –

The increasing knowledge of love

It is as we know Christ at home in the heart that we can go deeper and deeper into His love. Paul says three things about His love.

Knowledge comes to those who already love; 'that you, being rooted and grounded in love, may have power to comprehend.' It is only when you love that you see, that you become sensitive. It is as we have our roots deep and our foundations firm in the love of Christ that we get to know more of that love.

Then, *it is knowledge that comes to us 'with all the saints'*.

Because you see, there is a dimension of the love of Christ that you never get to know on your own. You only get to know it within the fellowship, within the company of God's people. We learn something of it from one another and share something of it with one another.

And it is, of course, *knowledge of something that surpasses knowledge*. It's like truth. It is given to all of us to see some of it, but it is given to none of us to see all of it. It is an ocean fullness, we can go on exploring it, but we will never exhaust it. Think of 'the breadth and the length and the height and the depth' of the love of Christ; how far it will stretch, how much it will stand, how low it will stoop and how high it will soar.

And then in verse 19 Paul prays for –

The incoming fullness of God

Paul prays that they may comprehend the love of Christ in such a way that they may be filled to the fullness of God; that is, that they may enjoy as much of the holiness and the wisdom and the grace and power of God as it is possible for a ransomed sinner to know.

When we pray for our churches, let us pray that they may know in experience the enabling power of the Spirit, the abiding presence of Christ, the increasing knowledge of love, the infilling fullness of God.

I feel that God is saying to us, as we have exposed our hearts to His Word, He is saying to us about our understanding of the truth, about our experience of love, about our commitment to ministry – 'wider; richer; fuller. I want you to have more!'

It's as if we said to the mouse in the cornfield, 'Eat and eat, there is always more.' It's as if we said to the fish in the sea, 'Drink and drink and go on drinking – there is always more.' It's as if we said to the bird in the air, 'Breathe and breathe and go on breathing, there is always more.' And God is saying to us about His love and His truth and His power, 'Take and take and go on taking – there is always more, for everybody, for ever!'

3 The Calling of the Church
(Ephesians 4:1-5:20)

It is said sometimes that the gospel is good news of what God has done, not good advice about what man must do. On the other hand, what God has done for us makes possible and indeed makes necessary what we are to do for Him. In other words, Christian duty presupposes Christian doctrine. Wasn't it Augustine who prayed, 'Give what Thou requirest, then ask what Thou wilt'?

The second half of the letter is a stirring call to holiness of life. It summons all who know the grace of God to work out what God has worked in. The section on Christian duty (chapters 4-6) can be divided into three sections: our calling, our conduct, and our conflict.

The calling of the Church (4:1-16)

We haven't time to look in detail at the New Testament doctrine of 'calling'. We are called *through the gospel* (2 Thessalonians 2:14); we are called *to the kingdom of God* (1 Thessalonians 2:12); and we are called *for fellowship and service*. Now there's an interesting thing – when Paul speaks about calling, he equates it with response. It's not only that the call of God is given to us, but that we respond to it. So what he writes here, at the beginning of the fourth chapter, has a reference to what the theologians term 'effectual calling', by which God so works in us that we are persuaded and enabled to embrace Jesus Christ as He is offered to us in the gospel.

Of course there is a sense in which you and I can never be worthy of the calling of God. You remember the story of the centurion who said, 'Lord, I am not worthy.' But it's interesting in the same chapter (Luke 7:3), that some of his friends, speaking to Jesus on his behalf, said of him, 'Lord, he is worthy; he is worthy to have You do this.' So Paul begins his call to Christian duty by begging us to be worthy of the calling. The word 'worthy' is an interesting one; it has two shades of meaning. It means first, 'to be of equal weight', the implication being that the Apostle wants us to have our doctrine and our behaviour in balance. On the other hand it means 'fitting', or 'proper'. He wants us to have a life that is becoming to the gospel we believe. Titus 2:10: 'with entire and true fidelity . . . they may adorn the doctrine of God our Saviour'. Tell me this morning – are you making a very real effort to 'adorn the doctrine' of which you love to speak?

Now Paul, in this section, speaks of the Church in two ways. First, he speaks of,

The unity of the Church (verses 2-6)
Our worthiness is tested within the fellowship of the Church. Our oneness with other Christians is an index to our oneness with Christ. Paul stresses unity, because it was God's plan to create a unity in Christ. We learn from verses 2 and 3 that this is a unity we must show. Certain qualities must be in evidence: lowliness (the self-forgetting of one who has a clear vision of himself in the sight of God), and meekness (the spirit of the Master who was 'meek and lowly in heart'). And then 'patient' – the word used to describe the longsuffering of Christ Himself. And 'forbearing one another in love'; not ceasing to love others because of faults in them which displease us. And manifesting these graces, we shall be 'eager to maintain the unity of the Spirit in the bond of peace.'

Now Paul makes a very strongly-worded appeal: 'Spare no effort to hold on to the unity you have.' We cannot *produce* this unity, but we must *protect* it. Unity in the church doesn't just happen; we must work at it. It is of course given by the Spirit: but it must be guarded by the saints. It is a unity we must show.

But it is also a unity we must know. We cannot show it unless we have it. Paul makes it clear that there is a unity which already exists for those who are in Christ, and he shows us in these verses that it has a threefold (or, looked at from another viewpoint, sevenfold) character.

Firstly it is *unity in the Spirit*. 'There is one body and one Spirit . . .' The Spirit's presence in our hearts is our passport to present membership in the Church and our pledge of a future inheritance in Christ. Then, it is *unity in the Son*; 'one Lord, one faith, one baptism . . .' What we may have here is a fragment of an early hymn, and certainly 'Christ is Lord' was the basic New Testament confession of faith. Faith focusses on the Lord, and baptism is the outward and visible sign.

It is *unity in the Father*: 'one God and Father above all . . .' He is above all people; He is king over angels, immortal, invisible, the only God, sovereign over all His people. He is the mighty one, who makes His people a dwelling place of God in the Spirit. In his book on Ephesians, John Stott writes: 'Is there only one God? Well then, He has only one Church. Is the unity of God inviolable? Then so is the unity of the Church. All parts of the true Church are one, in that they share a common life and own a common Lord.' But expression must be given to the common unity, and that is why Paul makes his appeal. You can't get it, but you can guard it. You must work at it.

And no divisions born of personal spleen or party spirit should be allowed to obscure the unity of the people of God. One of the sad things about evangelical life in this country, I think, is the way we suspect and oppose one another, even as evangelical Christians. You cannot take the teaching of this letter seriously and have those attitudes. If some of us are passionately against forms of unity which we feel to be unbiblical, then we must be equally passionately for those forms of unity which are biblical. Paul has in mind something more fundamental than just two happy weeks here in a tent at Keswick. Edward Carnell wrote: 'A spirit of divisiveness is never prompted by the Holy Spirit. For love is the law of life, and love remains unsatisfied until all who form the Body of Christ are united in a sacred fellowship.'

'Oh!' you say, 'an impossible ideal, with all our fragmentation and our denominations!' Yes; but so is our sanctification an impossible ideal. We know we will never achieve perfect oneness of the Church this side of heaven – but it must be the goal towards which we strive. We must continually set our hearts on this. If we are one, then we must be working and praying for the day when we shall be seen to be one. So let's not write off this whole question of the unity of the Church, as if it didn't matter.

The diversity of the Church (verses 7-16)

The unity of the Church is not a drab, colourless uniformity, but one which expresses itself in a rich diversity. The God who made all His stars different, and gave an individual design to each flower, makes His Church like that. He doesn't want us to conform to a stereotype. He wants to display His creative power in making us different! Paul here thinks of the Church as a body, and as the organs of a body differ in function while contributing to the whole, so do the members of the Church. Indeed, the Church only grows towards maturity when each member uses his gifts in the interest of the whole.

The subject of spiritual gifts is much discussed today. Note what Paul has to say in verses 7-11. Certain things are said about the gifts. First: *they are the gifts of Christ*. Paul quotes Psalm 68, which depicts the Lord returning in triumph with His captured foe. He applies what was said of the Lord Jehovah in the Old Testament to Christ. He sees Christ as taking captive His enemies, leading them in the train of triumph, and then bestowing them to the Church. It is only when Christ subdues and captures us that we can become faithful servants of His kingdom; captured by Christ, in order to be given to His Church, for service. I take the reference in verse 9 to be to the incarnation, when he 'emptied Himself, taking the form of a servant ... and became obedient unto death.' In His ascension God has highly exalted Him, and given Him a name which is above every name. William Barclay says of this, 'The ascension of Christ means not a Christ-deserted world, but a Christ-filled world.'

So then; all the gifts are the gifts of the Christ who lived and died and rose again to save us. If you have a gift, something which qualifies you for service, then you can no more claim credit for it than you can for the colour of your eyes. Your gift is the gift of Christ.

And then, they are *the gifts given to every Christian*. No-one has all the gifts; no-one is without a gift. Here he specifies some of the gifts, or gifted people, given to the Church. I take it that in this passage, Paul refers to the apostles and prophets, as founder-members of the Church. The apostles were specially chosen and commended, as eye-witnesses of the resurrection. The prophets were gifted with inspired utterances to make known the will of God to His people at a time when the New Testament writings were still being written. Evangelists on the other hand were the rank-and-file missionaries, men who went about sharing the good news. Pastor-teachers (I believe the two words refer to one function) were the ministers of the local church, engaged in day to day building up of the body of Christ.

Of course there are other gifts mentioned in the New Testament – in Romans 12, in 1 Corinthians 12 and 14 and also in 1 Peter. But let me say this. We are not to question or covet another's gift. Our responsibility is to exercise the gift that has been given to us. They are gifts given for the Church, not for our own enjoyment but for the Church's enrichment; as Paul puts it in verse 12. We should omit the first comma, and read it (with the New English Bible) as 'gifts are given ... to equip God's people for work in His service, to building up the body of Christ.' In other words: ministers such as these are given to the Church not in order to exercise their ministry but to enable and equip the members of the Church to exercise theirs.

How is the body built up? When all the members play their God-given part. Speaking of the equipping or perfecting of the Church, Paul uses a word which is found in the Gospels in Matthew 4:21, in the phrase 'mending their nets'. Why do fishermen repair nets? So that they can catch fish! If you are in the Church, if you're being fed, taught, helped, encouraged, it is in order to help you to fulfil your ministry. And what is envisaged here is the ministry of the whole people of God. We talk very often in our evangelical circles, don't we, about 'the priesthood of all believers'. Well – let's balance that by talking about the ministry of all believers, reminding ourselves that it is our privilege to talk to people on behalf of God.

You can see that Paul has a very high doctrine of the Church. It does not leave any of us the option of being a freelance Christian. Are you an 'unattached Christian', not attached to a local fellowship? You're not allowed to be like an isolated hand, or a spare foot dancing down the road and going nowhere in particular. You're a member of the body! And you must be seen to be a member.

Now in this passage the Apostle speaks to us not only of the gifts Christ gives to us but also of the growth Christ seeks in us. Look at verses 13-16. The Church, as we saw in our previous study, is in the course of construction. It must advance to maturity. Do you notice, in verse 13, that faith and knowledge go hand in hand? Here is the first mark of growth; *maturity in faith and knowledge*. Many churches, like many Christians, go through a protracted childhood. Can it be because, as Dick Lucas once suggested, they (like the Corinthian church) have baby pastors who serve only baby food? There are churches where you look in vain for adult Christianity. They're still at the ABC stage. But we're meant to stretch our minds in getting to grips with the Word of God!

Verse 14 is emphatic because this is such a recurring problem in the Church. And in it, Paul introduces us to a second mark of spiritual growth: *stability*. Isn't it amazing – and sometimes agonizing – how often Christians can be carried away by unbiblical teaching – the kind of teaching that is purveyed by false teachers, whose aim is to hoodwink the people of God! What is the remedy? It is found in verses 15 and 16. Paul uses the interesting, and virtually untranslatable, phrase, 'truthing it in love'. The Amplified

Bible attempts to unfold the meaning: 'speaking truly, dealing truly, living truly'. Now truth and love, like two elements innocuous when separated but unleashing a powerful energy when combined, have tremendous potential for growth when they are working together.

The conduct of the Church (4:17-6:9)

Paul's emphasis in the whole of this section is on the need for obedience. The Christian life is to be a life of separation (4:17-24). Every trace of the old life must be cast aside. Paul says (verse 17), 'You must no longer live as the Gentiles lived.' There were certain things they left behind when they became Christians; and Paul here gives us another ruthless picture (verses 18 and 19) of the kind of life from which Christ is excluded. That's life in the world. That's life without Christ. That's life in sin. And here you have a telling diagnosis of our permissive society. It is the product not of enlightenment, but of estrangement from God. And the only way to remedy that kind of life is to have men reconciled to God. Anything else doesn't work.

So now that these people were in the Church, there were things that they had left behind, but there were also things that they had learned (verses 20 and 21). What had changed them was Christ, and the truth about Him that they had learned from the Apostle. Again we have the typical Pauline emphasis on knowledge of the truth, recalling our Lord's words, 'You shall know the truth, and the truth shall make you free.'

But what was this truth that they had learned? Verse 22. Now Paul nowhere suggests (as some have argued) that the old nature has been left behind once and for all. He does not say that Christians have put off the old and put on the new with a single once-for-all commitment. He is describing the continual process of renewal – something necessary at every stage of our Christian development. As William Hendricksen puts it in his commentary, 'Their basic conversion had to be followed by a daily conversion.' Do you recognise that? Constantly leaving the old behind, constantly reaching out for the new. They had learned, as the New English Bible reads, that 'leaving your former way of life, you must lay aside that old human nature which, deluded by its lusts, is sinking down towards death.'

In a very real sense, the old life ends and a new one begins at our conversion, because if anyone is in Christ, there is a new creation. But the new man may go on wearing the old clothes. You and I as Christians must see to it, if we have been made new in Christ, that we adorn ourselves in the glorious dress Christ has provided for us. When a person marries, they become a new person and must live a life consistent with the new relationship into which they have entered. Paul says here, 'Be renewed in the spirit of your mind'; you must adopt a new way of thinking that will lead continually to a new way of living (verse 24).

Then in the long section running from 4:25 to 5:20, Paul says that the Christian life is a life of imitation. Children learn by imitating their parents; Christians must learn by imitating Jesus Christ. We've time only to look at this briefly. It means, first of all, walking in love. Paul gives here four blunt commands; and I don't think I can leave this out. Listen to this; 'Christians! *No more lying*!' (verse 25). Loving your neighbour involves telling him the truth; and remember, lying can include speaking what we do not know to be true as well as speaking what we know to be untrue. It also means there will be no flattery nor slander in our speech, and both are very common – even in Christian circles.

No more sulking (verses 26 and 27). Paul has in mind the fit of temper that subsides into a smouldering resentment fostered by wounded pride. Some of the old Greeks used to say, 'Shake hands before sunset'; and it's good advice for Christians, not least within the home. Harbouring grudges gives the devil a foothold. You remember how Cain's brooding anger led him to kill his brother. And *no more stealing* (verse 28). I was talking to an official in Belfast who was telling me of the number of people who do not pay electric bills, television licences and so on, and in an aside he said to me, 'And you can take it from me that there are a lot of Christians among them.' Do we pay our debts? Are we refusing to make false claims? Are we above-board in all our business transactions?

And *no more bad language* (verse 29). The Americans sometimes have a good way of putting things; I saw this on a poster outside a church building. 'Do be careful! Your tongue is in a wet place, it can easily slip.'

A life of imitation: walking in love. And Paul goes on in 5:3-14 to speak of 'walking in the light'. Certain things are excluded when we walk in the light, certain unmentionable sins and attitudes; and certain other things are created. I would encourage you to take up this section and see what the Apostle says about it. If we are to walk with Jesus Christ, we are to walk imitating the love that He showed. We are to walk in the light as He walked in the light – because, you remember, Jesus not only said 'I am the Light of the world,' but He said to His disciples, 'You are the light of the world.'

Could it be that in these days at Keswick some light will be kindled or rekindled, and we shall issue out into the Midlands, and the South, and the North, and out into the wider world, to shine: to shine for Jesus Christ, so that people may see our good works and glorify our Father who is in heaven? May it be so, for His name's sake.

4 Life in the Spirit
(Ephesians 5:21-6:24)

In the second part of this letter, Paul has been indicating some of the kinds of evidence in daily life that will mark us out as belonging to Christ. He shows us that we are called to a life of separation and a life of imitation, and we looked at the way in which this life, bearing the image of God Himself, involves walking in love and walking in light. Now, let me take you a further stage on the basis of 5:15-20, where Paul talks about walking in wisdom. 'Look carefully then how you walk, not as unwise men but as wise.'

Light is a symbol not only of purity, but also of knowledge and wisdom. Paul has said in 1:9 that this wisdom has been given to the Church, and in 1:17 he prays that the Church might have the spirit of wisdom. Now he urges them to walk in it, to live in it. You see, it is possible to have knowledge without wisdom. Some people are like that; they have only knowledge. But for Paul, wisdom is part-knowledge; part-knowledge of God.

Walking in wisdom (5:15-20)

Wisdom is shown in various ways. First (verse 16), it is shown in *the right use of time*. 'Make the most of' here involves acquiring time, by genuine effort and at real cost. You make time by sacrificing less important things for more important things. Less time for the daily newspaper: more time for the Bible. Less time for TV: more time for prayer. Thus we are to buy up the opportunities. Time cannot be recalled, it can only be redeemed.

Second, we show it by *our devotion to the will of God* (verse 16, 17). The word he uses for 'foolish' means 'stupid' or 'witless'. Don't be stupid; the will of God is the Christian's top priority. You display a God-given wisdom as you seek out and take to heart and apply to your life the will of God.

And then wisdom is shown by our response to the Holy Spirit (verse 18). I want to say two things here. Firstly, there is:

A contrast to be observed

– Between those who are drunk with wine and those who are filled with the Spirit. Wine was often used to induce the ecstasy of pagan worship; and all too often, under its influence, people could work themselves up into an emotional fervour which could lead to moral laxity. But Paul had also in mind what happened on the day of Pentecost, when there must have been at least a superficial resemblance between men filled with the Spirit and men drunk with wine. The word used for 'debauchery' is the word meaning 'dissipation', which is used elsewhere of the prodigal son. So Paul contrasts the intoxication of the drunkard with the exhiliration of the Spirit-filled Christian. And it's a marked contrast. Life in the Spirit is not reckless, but balanced. It is not wasteful but creative. It does not exhaust but enriches. The Holy Spirit, as A W Tozer says, is the cure for fanaticism, never its cause.

On the other hand we must not miss this point. There was something so distinctive, so singular about those Spirit-filled Christians on the day of Pentecost, that the men of the world said when they saw it, 'These men are full of new wine.' And I simply want to pause to ask you this question: Have our lives got such a buoyancy, such a joyful exuberance that we are marked out as those who live in the Spirit?

But not only is there a contrast to be observed, there is also

A command to obey

How do we speak of those who are filled with wine? We say that they are 'under the influence'; and this is Paul's command (verse 18). 'Be under the influence of the Holy Spirit.' It's not something optional, it is obligatory. It is God's will for us. Hence Paul puts it in the form of a command. Now we notice in passing three things about the command, 'Be filled'.

Firstly, *it is passive in form*. 'Let the Holy Spirit fill you', as the New English Bible translates it. Any reluctance is our responsibility, not God's. This of course does not mean that we are to be passive in our attitude to the Holy Spirit. A man gets drunk by drinking; so, we are to be filled with the Spirit by taking what God gives. That's the point made in the memorable words of John 7:38: 'If any man thirst, let him come to Me . . .' Our part is to believe, to thirst, to come, to drink. God's part is to bestow, to give the fullness we desire.

Secondly, *the word is plural*. It is addressed not to an individual but to the whole people, the whole Church. It's not something reserved for the few but something required of all. The Holy Spirit is not a luxury but a necessity. The Church can only be the Church as it lives in the fullness of the Spirit of God.

Thirdly, *the word is in the present tense*. It should properly read, 'Be ye being filled . . . go on being filled'. There is no reference to a once-for-all acceptance of what God gives. It denotes a habitual acceptance. One can distinguish, I realise, between the initial filling of the Spirit and the continual filling of the Spirit. There is a point at which the fullness begins – but there is also a process in which it continues.

So what happens when we allow the Spirit of God to fill us and go on filling us? Paul points out two immediate effects.

Firstly, he says, *it stimulates our worship* (verse 19). This worship, of course, is not simply a matter of addressing one another. It also involves singing and making melody in our heart to the Lord. How often we forget that, in church life! The biblical concept of worship is of something that minister and people offer together to God. He is the audience.

Therefore worship is never a performance offered to people. At the centre of such worship will be a spirit of thanksgiving (verse 20). Thanksgiving is always the other side of the mercy. So, as God offers us this grace through Jesus Christ, it is fitting that we should offer Him our gratitude through Jesus Christ.

Secondly, the fullness of the Spirit comes *to stimulate our worship*, and then it comes *to regulate our fellowship*. Notice the sequence: speaking to one another; singing with one another; submitting to one another (verse 21). What would you say is the chief hindrance to right relationships in church life? Self-centredness, surely; a disease of which there are many symptoms. But when the Holy Spirit comes, He makes us open to one another, He makes us willing to prefer one another, He enables us to submit to one another. The chief remedy for our self-centredness is adoration of God. Only as we are lifted up out of ourselves into vital fellowship with God can we have healthy and harmonious fellowship with one another.

In all this, Paul is anxious to show that the filling of the Holy Spirit is not given in order to make us feel good, but in order to make us live well. He does not come in order that we may exalt ourselves. He comes in order that we may subject ourselves. And that is a test of His working.

We have seen that as Christians we are called to a life of separation; and to a life of imitation. Now, Paul reminds us that life in the Spirit is also a life of obligation.

A life of obligation (5:21-6:9)

Here the Apostle gives three down-to-earth illustrations of how life in the Spirit is to be lived out in the workaday world. How much does your experience of Christ show itself in your home life? And isn't it significant, that Paul says not only that we are to be 'filled with the Spirit', but that we are to be 'subject to one another out of reverence for Christ'? Just as in an army where soldiers are subject not only to their commanding officers but also to their comrades; so a Christian who is subject to Christ will also be subject to his fellow-Christians in the home, in the church and outside. We are not free to go our own way, to do our own thing. And Paul shows how this selfless subjection will apply in three different areas.

Wives and husbands (5:22-33)

There is a pattern presented here. The husband/wife relationship must be understood in the light of the relationship between Christ and the Church. In verse 25, notice how the New Testament centres both doctrines and practice in the cross. The Apostle stresses the selfgiving love of Christ for the Church, and, by implication, the submission of the Church to Christ. And how are we brought into submission to Him?

> O Lord, I yield, I yield,
> I can hold out no more.
> I sink, by dying love compelled
> To own Thee conqueror.

He is Master, because first of all He is Saviour. His headship is a headship of love. It is in the light of this that we must understand Paul's words, 'The husband is the head of the wife as Christ is the head of the Church.'

Now there is a practice commanded here. 'Wives, be subject to your husbands, as to the Lord.' How are we to understand this? Does it mean that the husband is the boss, and the wife the slave? Two phrases are significant. 'Be subject to one another out of reverence for Christ.' 'To your husbands be subject as to the Lord.'

Keep in mind what Christ is! Remember not only His sovereign claim, but His selfgiving love. Remember His leadership is not something forcibly imposed, but something willingly accepted.

The wife will show her devotion to her husband as to one who loves her as he loves his body. The husband is not superior in rank to his wife; but he has a different role. As in a committee all members may be equal but the chairman has a specific authority which must be recognised, so in a home husband and wife are equal partners, yet he has a special authority and responsibility. So much so, that Paul can say 'The husband is the head of the wife.' Part of his responsibility is normally to make provision for the home and to give direction to the home.

And now the husband is counselled in his turn (verse 25). Paul here uses the distinctive word for love which indicates a holy, unselfish love – one which never insists on its 'rights' or merely seeks its own satisfaction. Christian love is one hundred per cent caring for the other person regardless of the cost to ourselves. And, Paul points out, it is a love that purifies and beautifies.

Now in all this teaching Paul shows two things I want to mention in passing. One is this. *Marriage involves a decisive step* (verses 28, 29, 31). A new entity comes into being at marriage. That is what makes it so decisive and binding. And Paul's stress on the union and intimacy of two people within the marriage bond shows why choosing a partner should be much less a matter of impulse and inclination, and much more a matter of prayer and principle. I want to say this to any young people here who may be still happily unmarried. At home I say to our young people: next only to the decision to follow Christ, is the decision you make about your partner in life. Be careful! It either makes or mars your life, this decisive step into marriage.

But secondly, *marriage involves an exclusive state*. A man is joined to his wife and the two shall become one (and I think we should say that no third party, no parent or in-law, should ever come between husband and wife. It does happen, even in Christian circles). The two are one. How sad that we find people, even in Christian circles, breaking the bond that God had sealed and rationalising the break when it comes. Only as we grasp the high New Testament ideal of marriage can we appreciate the force of Paul's statement in 1 Corinthians 6:9, and it's very solemn word: 'Do not be deceived; neither the immoral, nor idolaters, nor adulterers, nor sexual perverts . . . will inherit the kingdom of God.' As Christians we must be on guard against sinful alliances. And let anyone who thinks that he stands, take heed lest he fall. Sometimes there can be a sinful and dangerous trifling with the feelings of others. We need to live in the Spirit if we are to be liberated from the things that endanger the marriage relationship.

Children and parents (6:1-4)
In his graphic picture of pagan Rome, Paul speaks of those who are 'disobedient to parents, foolish, faithless, heartless, ruthless' (Romans 1:31). In contrast, then, life in the Spirit is a controlled, rightly adjusted life with a proper balance of rights and responsibility. We live in a society where there is a tremendous emphasis on 'rights'. We want our rights in the home, at work, in the wider life of society; but we don't hear so much about responsibility.

To children, Paul says 'Obey your parents in the Lord.' And he gives three reasons.

'*Do it for it is right*' – that is, it is a law of nature for the parent to direct and the child to obey.

'*Do it in the Lord*' – for the child of a Christian home has a covenant relationship with the Lord. And in such a home the parents represent the Lord to the child. The father is the symbol of authority.

'*Do it (for this is the first commandment with a promise) that it may be well with you and that you may live long on the earth.*' We may in fact take it that this is the first commandment with a promise – a promise, if I may suggest this, not to be taken in an individualistic sense but as stating the general principle that a society in which children honour their parents is a society that will enjoy greater stability and prosperity. We obey our parents as we show respect for them, as we make provision for them, and as we yield submission to them. Young people – are you bearing this in mind? This is the life in the Spirit. This is how it works out.

But to fathers, Paul says verse 4. I like the New English Bible's rendering of this: 'Give them the instruction and the correction that belong to a Christian upbringing.'

There is a happy mean between over-indulgence and over-severity. Fathers in the first century tended to be over severe. Martin Luther tells us that his father was so hard and harsh that he himself found it very difficult to refer to God as 'Father'. On the other hand, we must not treat an adolescent like a mere child. And we must be scrupulously fair and avoid every trace of favouritism with our children. We must never administer punishment when our own temper is out of control. If the child is to respect the parent, then the parent must earn that respect; not by wielding the big stick, but by being the person he or she is. The object of wise training is to get the child to accept for him or herself the standards you set, to assimilate them into their own character. If you imposed standards forcibly, the child will reject them as soon as he's out of your reach.

And could I also say this? Christian parents, in their desire for the welfare of their children, can sometimes turn them into little too-good-to-be-true prigs. Don't make your child into something unnatural. And remember this, nothing puts a teenager off the Christian faith so much as the parent who is a professing Christian, but in whose life at home there is little evidence of the fruit of the Spirit. No-one sees through camouflage so clearly as a child.

Let William Hendricksen sum up this counsel of the Apostle in this way. 'The very heart of Christian nurture is to bring the heart of the child to the heart of the Saviour.'

Slaves and masters (6:5-9)

Obviously, when Paul turns to speak about slaves and masters, he is still thinking about the Christian household. He does not call on Christian masters to free their slaves, but (as Hendricksen says) 'he took the social situation as he found it, and endeavoured by peaceful means to change it.'

We haven't time to deal with this in detail. But what Paul required of slaves and servants was that they should be reliable. Reliable to their immediate masters, reliable to God Himself; that they would do their work as unto the Lord. But, balancing that, masters were required to be responsible (verse 9). God treats the master and his men equally and impartially, and the relationship between the two must be worked out in the light of that fact.

Now let me spend the remainder of our time saying something about Christian conflict.

To live under the influence of the Spirit, facing up to the standards God has set for us, will inevitably lead to conflict with the devil and his hosts. So Paul finishes this letter with what we may call,

Battle orders (6:10-13)

Let us remember this: the Church contends with forces operating behind the scenes (verse 12), forces which are almost invincibly armed. But – and this, we must never forget – Christ has been invested with a power that has placed Him far above all rule and authority and power and domination, not only in this age but in that to come. Not only so; but He has disarmed the principalities and powers and made a public spectacle of them, triumphing over them at the cross. So let us remember this, that while we face our relentless foe, we face a defeated foe, and we must stand on the ground of Christ's victory. Two things about Satan's attacks are to be noted. One, their *subtlety* (verse 11). Compare this with 4:14, where the Apostle has already spoken of the 'deceitful wiles' of the devil's angels. The arch-deceiver uses every subterfuge and strategem to ensnare the people of God; now masquerading as an angel of light, now on the rampage as a roaring lion. So, as Paul says in 2 Corinthians 2:11, we have to be on our guard all the time. He is a wily foe.

But note also the *suddenness* of his attacks (verse 16). We know that in primitive warfare, darts tipped with pitch were ignited and then hurled against the enemy in a surprise attack. So the Apostle warns us against the sudden onslaught that comes upon us like a bolt from the blue.

In such a battle, we have no strength of our own. I don't care how long you have been a Christian, I don't care how mature you are, I don't care how many battles you have fought and won; you are never a match in your own strength for warfare against Satan.

The armour with which we are equipped (6:14-20)

Our time is gone. But I want to say two things about this armour in general.

First of all, *the armour described here is armour for the whole army*. It is what God gives His people to equip them for the fray. A solitary soldier going out to fight the enemy would be ridiculous. The Romans were so effective in war because of their corporate manoeuvres. And I want you to remember this: none of us has been called to fight alone. We fight in company with the whole people of God. We need each other. We must strengthen each other. We must stand with each other. It's very sad in a Christian fellowship when you find people fighting one another. We must stand together, to fight the foe.

Secondly, *Christ Himself is the armour*. He is truth, He is our righteousness, He is our gospel of peace. He is our shield of faith, He is our salvation, He is the living Word of God. And we must lay hold of Him in prayer. As we open our hearts to His generous influence, as we allow Him to arm us for the fight, then we shall be fitted for the battle.

Make no mistake. If you've been blessed and helped in this Convention, as soon as you're back home the warfare will come at you, the devil will be all out to undermine your experience, to make you content with the same old low-level standard of Christian living. You need Jesus Christ. You need to be clothed with Jesus Christ. You need to stand complete in Him. Only then will you fight and win.

And so, the Apostle brings this great letter to an end with a greeting. Verses 21 and 22 remind us of how Paul had the knack of attracting to himself staunch friends, firing them with his own vision and zeal. He was a great human, more concerned for others than himself, so he sends his colleague to give the Ephesians up-to-date news of his situation, 'that you may know how we are, and that you may encourage your hearts.'

He finishes with the blessing, a blessing which underscores the prominent words used throughout the letter.

Peace – peace with God, peace within the fellowship, peace in their own hearts.

Love – love for God, love for one another, love undying for the Lord Jesus.

Grace – the most basic blessing of all, the fount from which everything else fittingly flows.

This is where the Apostle leaves us: the grace with which our sovereign Lord comes to save us. The grace by which He makes us part of His Body, the Church. The grace by which He makes it possible for us to live in true holiness, to fight and to overcome, and all of this is received increasingly in the open hand of faith.

And again and again, we're reminded of this. All is by His grace. Nothing comes from us. Everything comes from Him, and all is for His glory. Nothing giving a lift to me, everything giving a lift to Him.

May you go out and live on that principle, by His grace, for His glory alone.

THE ADDRESSES

'I WILL POUR OUT MY SPIRIT'

by Rev Philip Hacking

Joel 2

It's a great joy to be with you at Keswick again. It's a delightful thing to be in Keswick. But – I wonder if we also realise that it is a very dangerous place to be?

That can be true in two ways. Firstly, I think we need to be aware that we can at Keswick be unduly cushioned against what's happening in our world outside. And I don't believe we are meant to be so cushioned.

But secondly, Keswick can be a dangerous place, in that God can work amongst us and start stirring us up. And in that sense, I trust that you are ready for danger; the Spirit's at work here in our tent this morning!

You see, there's always the problem that in a sense, we would want to say, the messages from Keswick are timeless. And you could find some of those addresses from a hundred years ago, and – in a sense – they won't have changed. But our world has changed; and in *that* sense, the timeless Word must be related to our world in which we live.

And the other problem at Keswick, I suggest, is that we might easily assume that here 'God speaks to me personally'. Now that's desperately important. You can hide behind a crowd, you can imagine He's speaking to others, but yes, it's right, He speaks to us, personally. But – at the same time – we are part of the world, and unless God does something in us today that's relevant not only to us but to our society, I believe that we have (again, in a sense) failed. It's with that in mind that I want us to turn to the book of the prophet Joel. I believe that he is saying something that's terribly relevant to us and to our world.

The interesting thing about Joel is that we have not the slightest idea when he preached. The critics argue and they differ by five hundred years between the earliest and the latest dates. Doesn't matter! We don't know any personal details about him except the name of his father, and that doesn't get you very far. His name was Pethuel, and more than that we do not know.

But two things we know about Joel. Firstly he preached in a day when there was a great swarm of locusts, and the land of which he was a part was devastated, and God was speaking. And the second thing we know is that on the day of Pentecost it was in the prophet Joel that Peter had his inspiration, and he preached that first ever pentecostal sermon on the phrase 'This is that which is spoken by the prophet Joel.'

Now don't you see? That's exactly what God wants to say to us today. Joel speaks a word of warning from God, he calls a nation to repentance. But at the same time, he offers us a tremendous hope, the hope of the Spirit of God to move amongst us.

If you look at Joel 2:3, a picture of that swarm of locusts and all the harm they were doing, I wonder if you think it may say something to us about the locusts that devour our nation just now; fire devours before them, and behind them a flame burns? As we see the riots on our streets, dare we believe that somehow, very specially, God is speaking to us through them? He actually calls the locusts (verse 25) 'My great army which I sent among you'. Many of us would want to stop at that. Here's Joel who dares to say that this devastating force moving through the land is actually God's great army which He has sent among them.

And I want to say, that I believe God is in control, and in His own sovereign way He's actually having to speak to us in a language we don't like. The prophet never baulks from saying it, and I dare not either.

But alongside that message of the locusts comes the great

promise of the Spirit of God. It's a wonderfully universal prophecy. It's about what He's going to do for all people. Look at verse 28 and verse 32; and in chapter 3 he talks more than once about 'all you nations'. Now surely you and I believe that what God did first at Pentecost and has been doing constantly in His Church and here in this tent, is not just for us – it's got a great universal reference. Has it ever struck you, when you think of what God did on the day of Pentecost, that He was doing the reverse of what He did with the Tower of Babel back in Genesis 11, when He confounded the language? On the day of Pentecost it was reversed, people from all nations heard in their own languages the wonderful works of God. That is the work of the Spirit; it's a world work.

And I want us to see that what God wants to do today is no trivial job. Sometimes I think we trivialise the Spirit. We haven't thought in terms of what He can do not just in my life, but to transform the world. We dishonour God if we imagine that somehow it's just for us. So listen to God saying through Joel, 'I will pour out My Spirit.' And I want to suggest that there are two promises, which I hope we will take to heart. And the first is,

The promise of God's grace in repentance

You might have a nice little debate (though mercifully, for folk like me, Keswick is not a debating ground) on what is meant by 'a prophetic word'. It becomes a kind of battle-ground! 'What is prophecy today?'

Well, if you're expecting me to enter into that debate in detail, I won't be doing so. But I want to say that all too often the prophetic word which is not heard is a word which speaks of the big things of God. Very often 'our God is too small'. The real prophetic word that comes from Joel is going to speak about what's happening on the streets of England and Northern Ireland and throughout the world. And what is God saying? Two things:

Listen to Me

If you are a parent, have you ever had the feeling when you talk to your children, that they're not listening? You're giving them a little lecture, you go on at great length and suddenly it dawns on you that though they stand silent they are not the slightest bit listening to you. Some of you who are teachers may have the same problem with your classes from time to time, and some of us who preach sometimes have the same problem with our congregations. If I were to suddenly come down and shake you by the shoulder, it might be because I thought you were not listening to me. And do you know, I think that God has to shake us sometimes and say, 'Are you listening to Me?'

And the Bible insists right through both Testaments, that if the people of God don't listen when he speaks through His prophetic Word, if we turn our backs, then He has to speak to us in ways we do not like. And I have no hesitation in saying that God is speaking loud and clear to a nation that by and large has shut its ears to His Word.

Notice in 1:15, that the swarm of locusts is to Joel a picture of the day of the Lord which is near. Look at 2:10: here is Joel seeing this terrible event as a picture of the great and final day of the Lord. Jesus does the same; He says to the people of His generation, Jerusalem will fall; and because you have not listened to Me, you will have to listen in the hour of judgement. And in 3:13 Joel says that God is going to put the sickle in, for the harvest is ripe; words that Jesus picks up in the parable of the wheat and tares. It bothers me that sometimes the note of urgency is being taken from the churches where it belongs and is being preached by very different people. Have you seen the Nuclear Disarmament sticker, which points to the minute before midnight? It reminds us, we haven't got long. And whatever your views on disarmament, that message is I think clear.

You ask any people in a survey what they expect. People are expecting disaster. They are expecting nuclear war. They are expecting judgement! And I believe that the Church of Jesus Christ ought to be reminding us that there is a day of Judgement, and we need to be alert to the hour in which we live. It would be a tragedy if Keswick were just Christian people hearing timeless truths, when our nation burns. We would be held responsible before God. I believe He's shaking us today and saying 'Listen to Me.' We haven't got long.

Turn to Me

When you listen to Me, says God (2:12-17), then I ask you to repent. The call to repentance is very interesting. When He calls us to repent in 2:12, we are to repent with all our heart, with fasting, with weeping and mourning. We need to get down to that place where it makes such a difference to us that we do shed tears about the sins of the world. We repent 'with all our heart', and the Hebrew has it right. The heart is not the seat of emotions though it is often said to be. The Hebrew knew that the heart is the seat of the emotion and the will. God isn't talking primarily about how you feel. He's talking about how you act and how you live. Something real and genuine. I'm impressed that when, on that day of Pentecost, Peter preached from Joel, he ended his sermon when the crowd cried, 'Men and brethren, what shall we do?' He said, 'Repent, and be baptised.' On the day of Pentecost! He didn't say, 'You know the Spirit's at work, it's wonderful, it's exciting; what a wonderful day it is – come and join us!' He said, 'Repent.' And oh, that that were heard. The need of our day is for no superficial moving, but a deep-seated revival.

'Turn to Me' – that is (2:15-17) all the people, including the leaders. I guess I speak to a number of folk who are setting the lead in different churches. I say to you, as I say to myself, we should be setting the lead in deep-seated repentance for our sins. I remember that when Isaiah was called to the work of prophecy, when he was aware of the sins of his nation, he didn't say 'Forgive them.' '*I* am a man of unclean lips, and *I* dwell in the midst of a people of unclean lips.' I wonder how many in our nation have decided just what's wrong, and how we'd put it right, and who's causing the trouble? God says it's you and me. When He begins to move, it's not 'them', it's 'us'! The real urgent need is repentance and renewal within the House of God, that we might go out with clean hands to a world that doesn't think the Church has got anything to say worth hearing.

The promise of God's gifts in abundance

I do not believe for one moment that Keswick is a place where we 'put the screws on'. But if God speaks of Jesus in such a way it brings about repentance, praise God. I don't know about you, but I have found that when I discover what God wants to do for me and give to me, I recognise my sin. Not because He puts the screws on me, but because I see how far short I fall, and what I was meant to be. I hope that's where some of us are; then we're ready for God's gifts in abundance.

Just two things the Lord offers us, through Joel.

Joel 2:18-27 is in a sense all about *a material bonus*. There's no doubt he is speaking of a restoration of prosperity that can be seen, that God's people can learn the secret of prosperity. I don't believe that as Christians we are meant to expect prosperity in that sense, but I do believe that here is the heart of the problem that affects our nation and many others. If we really want to know what God wants to pour out on us, it'll only be ours as we repent. 'I will restore the years that the locust has eaten' – Joel is promising that when a people turn back to God they have all that they need and enough and to spare. And I believe if only we, as God's people, would learn to give and to sacrifice, God would bless us. I wonder if it is the case that some of us hold back and will never know the joy.

But the main offer that Joel brings us is not just a material bonus, but *a spiritual surplus*. We'll dwell on that for the remainder of our time together. I hope we will go out with our appetites whetted for what God would give to us. Is it not true, that man's necessity is God's opportunity? That because our nation has reached almost the depths (we really couldn't ever credit, some of us, that it could get like this) that we've reached the place where we look with expectancy for what God's going to do?

In Acts 4, you get an amazing picture of the disciples up

before the Sanhedrin, in danger of their lives. They start to pray something like this: 'Lord, look on their threats; give us boldness to preach; and then – and then, Lord, You stretch forth Your hands, and do signs and wonders, in the name of Your holy servant Jesus.'

The prayer I instinctively *want* to pray is, 'Lord, just look at the mess we're in. Lord, just deliver us from it all. Lord, help us to go on and live a nice easy and comfortable life.' But I daren't pray it; God won't let me. And so I pray, 'Lord, look at the mess we're in ... give us courage to go out with boldness and give us grace to expect that in the midst of all this, You'll do something new. You'll revolutionise us. You'll set the world upside down, because you set the Church upside down.' Dare you pray like that? Many of us just want ease and comfort, we don't like being disturbed. Many of us only begin to feel when it hits us.

Our new curate in my church made a very profound observation. He was doing his first hospital visiting. He said he was talking to an old gentleman who was really bothered about the problem of suffering, really rebellious against God. Here was a man, said our curate, who was well on into his seventies – and had clearly never bothered to think about these things before. He had lived in our world with all its suffering and tension, and hadn't agonised; and then he and his wife were taken ill. Then it was: Why does God let it happen?

Can you imagine anybody, living in our world until their seventies, and never bothering? Yes! Because it's only when it comes onto our streets that some of us begin to realise the enormity of it.

Therefore I want to pray: 'Lord, this is the hour; don't just keep us comfortable, don't just make it easier for us; give us grace to believe that You are going to do new things.' What things? Well, here's the spiritual surplus.

The promise of the surplus comes in a mighty passage, 2:28 – the promise of the outpouring of the Spirit. Find time to read and meditate on that verse. Take time to digest it.

Firstly, *it's a promise of an outpouring.* 'I will pour out My Spirit on all flesh.' I was very impressed as I studied

Scripture on the work of the Spirit. How often that phrase comes. It's there in Isaiah 32:15. It's there in John 7, when Jesus promises that out of our innermost being will flow rivers of living water. 1 Corinthians 12, 13: we are to be baptised in, to drink in the Spirit. Don't you see? A kind of abundance, a filling, an overflowing. Therefore the promise of Joel, picked up on the day of Pentecost. It's not just that somehow, the Church will go on; but that we'll spill out. I don't want to belong to a Church that just 'survives'; I hope that the churches will be revived; and that's the promise of the Spirit – an outpouring of His Spirit.

Notice, secondly, *it is a promise for everybody.* 'I will pour out My Spirit on all flesh.' 'Well,' said Peter, 'look; it's happened.' And, you'll notice, everybody could share it. Oh! Moses longed for it way back in Numbers 11 – 'I wish that all God's servants were prophets, and that God would pour out His Spirit on all God's people' – different gift, but the same Spirit, the same fruitage, the same possibilities. Is your church, is my church, a place where I can honestly say that all God's children are exercising their God-given right to be filled with the Spirit and overflow? Would it not be fair to say, that if the Church of Jesus in the past twenty-five years had been living like this, some of the things over which we shake our heads today might never have come to pass? I believe it, with all my heart.

Then, would you notice another thing. I'm always interested that when Peter quoted Joel 2 he didn't stop at verse 29. You might have thought he would. But he went on to talk about the events of 2:30-32. Why? Some would say – and who am I to deny the possibility – that what verse 32 says is that before the Lord returns there'll be one great massive world revival. May it be so! I'm not sure if that's exactly what this verse says, but if that's what it does say, I would be delighted to acknowledge it.

But I believe that what it is reminding us of is that the climax of these new and mighty things God is doing – Jesus' death, resurrection and ascension – will be Christ's return. And is it not *this* that we want to say to our world, with all its need; the only sure fact of the future of our world is that

Jesus returns? There is going to be that great day of the Lord. And we're not promised that it will be prefaced by ease and comfort. He did talk about wars and rumours of wars. So we go out to that situation with a word not of easy optimism but of hope. And the pouring of the Spirit is a proof of the final day of Jesus. How do you know He's coming back? That you will be with Him? Because He's promised. And the great fulfillment of His promise here and now is the gift of the Spirit.

More than once, Paul speaks of the Spirit as an 'earnest' – you've come across that word; in modern Greek, the word for an 'earnest' is the word for an engagement ring. It's a lovely picture. When a young lady receives an engagement ring, she's delighted – but not satisfied. She's looking for the day when there'll be a second ring. The one ring says that the other ring will come.

I hope that as a Christian with the Spirit, you're delighted but not satisfied. Until heaven comes, there will always be something that is, in a sense, missing. I believe we are wrong to assume that everything is like a package deal that we have now. There's a glorious 'not yet'. There is a glorious thing that will only be in the glory of heaven. There are many things I'll never know till then. Until the resurrection of the body I shall never know complete freedom from pain and suffering. And there are many other things – 'only then . . .' – but the Spirit's a proof.

As far as the world is concerned, there will be wars and rumours of wars. There will always be tensions, but there's a great 'then' that we can proclaim. And there's one more thing from Joel. In 3:18, he promises that what happens with the people of God will become like something flowing out to the rest of the world. Ezekiel says exactly the same thing: a vision of the House of God, out of which flows the river of living water. I don't imagine that the national Press would ever think that the fact of a few thousand people meeting at Keswick has the slightest relevance to what's happening in our nation. They might even say cynically, 'Isn't that typical? Christians just run away, into their little escapist ghettos, into the beautiful Lake District, and it's got nothing to do with what's happening on our streets.' I understand what they think, and, sadly, I would have to say that they are sometimes right. But they ought not to be. For if the Spirit moves amongst us, then, you see, what happens amongst us can be flowing out to the world.

The very last verse of the book of Joel is quite simple. 'The Lord dwells in Zion.' And when the Spirit of the Lord moves in the people of God, then here in our midst is a reality which we believe is bound to affect the world outside. There are no slick answers. But we have in the promise of God through Joel the supreme answer to the needs of our society. And it starts with the people of God.

Do you really believe that God is speaking to us today as much by what's happening on the streets of Brixton and everywhere else as by what's happening in the tents at Keswick? Do you really believe God speaks like that? And if you are only half listening to that message, isn't God saying 'Repent, turn to Me with all your heart?' If He is saying that to us, are we ready and willing to see God so revolutionise us that it's bound to affect the world?

The mark of what the Spirit is doing in our churches is, in some Christians' minds, to do with worship, with feelings, with sharing, with happiness. Thank God for these; but, please friends, the world outside is not changed by that. The world outside is only changed when the Spirit of God goes a lot deeper and transforms us. 'I will pour out My Spirit' – Lord, we need it so much. Come amongst us! Turn us to Yourself; make us channels of Your blessing.

'THE WORDS ON OUR TONGUES'

by Rev George Duncan

Psalm 139:4

The little phrase on which I want to base our thinking takes me away back to a time when I sat in the audience at Keswick. I was wearing a kilt! I was a scoutmaster, and we were camping on the side of Latrigg, on Windy Brow. Among the speakers then was one of the most lovely men, I think, ever to have graced this platform, the American, S.D. Gordon. His books were all entitled *Quiet Talks on . . .*, and he himself never raised his voice above a whisper. He did not raise his voice to emphasise a point, he lowered it; 'Are you listening?' he would say, scarcely audibly, and we would sit up to hear what he had to say.

He took a study on Psalm 139. I remember he said that there were two kinds of searching; the search of the law (which is what happens when there's a knock on the door, and you open it, and a policeman with a search warrant is standing there); and the search of love (he took the analogy of a mother greeting a son who has been away from home for some time, searching his face to see if he's come back all right). And in the detail of this lovely psalm which has to do with the searching love of God, comes this phrase in verse 4: 'There is not a word in my tongue, but lo, O God, Thou knowest it altogether.'

I have three headings. The first is, that here we are dealing with

Something intensely practical

There are two reasons. Firstly, we are all daily involved. A tongue is something we all have and use daily. Nothing could be more practical than that. God is concerned and knows about the words on our tongue; that is the Psalmist's claim. Secondly, we find that not only are we daily involved, but God is deeply concerned. I wonder whether we give enough thought to this? The Scriptures have so much to say on the importance of what we say and how we say it. Proverbs 6:16 lists those things most distasteful to the heart of God, and two or three have to do with the tongue: a lying tongue, a false witness, he that soweth discord. The Psalmist says (39:1) 'I will take heed unto my ways that I sin not with my tongue' – I can sin with my tongue – and our text says, 'There is not a word in my tongue but lo O God Thou knowest it altogether.'

Maybe God will bring us to a new awareness of the importance of our tongues and our words. This is nothing airy-fairy. It affects me in the home, what I say there, how I say it. It affects children and parents, husbands and wives, because we talk to one another. It touches us when we work, because we talk there. The only place when maybe it does not affect us is when we sleep – though some of us even talk in our sleep!

You see what a very tremendous thing this is. It brings the whole question of Christian living and holiness, if you like to use that word, to touch everyone, everything; to involve us all the time, anywhere. Something intensely practical.

Something immensely powerful

The second thing has a note of encouragement and also a note of warning. We are dealing with something immensely powerful.

When James talks about the tongue, he uses six different things to illustrate his point. Two of them illustrate our heading. The tongue is immensely powerful. In his third chapter he says the tongue is a 'little member'. It seems unimportant, but it is immensely powerful – why? Because it is like the bit in the horse's mouth, like the rudder in a ship. He is talking of the way our words can direct our life. You and I are not to think of them as insignificant. I do not think anybody was very much bothered when back in 1924 a fifteen-year-old schoolboy asked his younger brother to go and hear a preacher. It was an unimportant triviality, unrecorded except in heaven. That younger brother was me, and my brother did not know when he invited me to go that God was going to bring me to Himself, and that in His incredible grace and mercy He would make me a preacher who would travel the world. Just a simple sentence: 'Will you come with me?' Immensely powerful.

Do you know, I think that this is one of the glories of the ministry of the Holy Spirit. When I read of the Holy Spirit's ministry, that He would testify to me of Christ, I always thought that it meant that He would testify *to me* of Christ – and I was right! But it doesn't stop there. He wants to testify *through me* as well, to others. And you see you do not need a three-point sermon for the Holy Spirit to use your words. Just a simple invitation to somebody to come to your church – when did you last ask anybody to come? If somebody comes to your neighbourhood, who has just moved in down the road, and they don't know anybody – do you, caring for them, seeing what has happened, go and call? Just as somebody once, brought a bramble-and-apple pie when we moved into the Vicarage at Cockfosters.

We have to realise that the sheer miracle of the ministry of the Holy Spirit is that the Lord likes to take things that seem insignificant, and use them in an immensely powerful way; to give direction to a life which that life never had before. And I believe that if ever there was a time when this vision to the Church was needed, that we become vocal in the expression of the mind of God, it is now. Why is it, that all the talking is done by others and the Church remains dumb? (Some of you may remember that two years ago here at Keswick I felt burdened to speak on 'The sin of silence'. 'We do not well: this is a day of good tidings, and we hold our peace.')[1]

Something immensely powerful – because of the direction our words can give to lives. I wonder how many lives? I think that this is going to be one of the exciting things about heaven, to discover how God has used a very simple little thing – a letter, a word. Don't wait for the big occasion, the big crusade. I am one hundred percent behind Billy Graham; God's time, God's place; but that is very unusual, such men come almost once in a generation – what is happening the rest of the time? God is counting on you and me, just where we are.

But the tongue is also immensely powerful because of the destruction our words can bring. James goes on in his illustrations to speak of fire and poison; both are destructive. That is why God is concerned with the words on my tongue, I wonder whether James has in his mind two kinds of destructive speaking?

One kind of destructive speaking is accidental, like a fire. Anyone who visits Australia knows the destruction that the bush fire can do. It can travel thirty, forty, fifty, sixty miles an hour; and so often, they are started accidentally. I have seen burnt-out shells of houses after a bush fire that started in a rubbish dump. When that bottle was left there in the rays of the sun, nobody knew it was going to ignite a piece of paper alongside and go on to devastate thousands of acres. No wonder God is deeply concerned about the words on my tongue, when H knows about their destruction.

I wonder how many people have had the beginnings of a feeling after Christ destroyed through the words on my tongue? I heard of an incident that happened in an office on a Monday morning. A business man had been involved in a Christian broadcast the night before, and a girl he employed had heard it. That morning he was in a very bad mood, things were not going well, and for some reason this girl got the benefit of his temper. As she went out of the office, she

1. *The Lord Is King: Keswick 1979* (ed. David Porter, STL Books, 1979), p.118

said to another girl who was coming in, 'That's right ...
Come to Jesus on Sunday night and go to hell on Monday
morning ...' Destruction! Do you think the girl would be
likely to be interested in Christian things after that? Our
Lord's searching words to the Pharisees were, 'Ye have taken
away the key of knowledge: ye entered not in yourselves, and
them that were entering in ye hindered' (Luke 11:52).

Sometimes we are foolish enough, perhaps, to sit down
and think of how many people we have led to the Lord. It's a
foolish exercise. You'll find out when you get to glory. Some
of you will get a wonderful surprise, you will find out how
many, through your giving, your praying and caring – the
names are there. But I wonder how many we have put off,
just because we snap, just because we're in a bad mood?
Christian nurse – you were desperately tired, God knew you
were tired, but that didn't excuse you speaking like that to
the patients ... Mum snapping, at the kids, maybe at Dad
arriving home ... The destruction our words can bring. It's a
familiar weapon used by our enemies; I read a book not long
ago by a man who had left Communism, and he wrote of the
smear campaigns and other verbal attacks made by the
extreme Left against their opponents. This tiny little
member in our mouths is something immensely powerful –
and when we think in terms of what the Holy Spirit can do
through what we say, powerful beyond anything.

But we find something else. Psalm 139 says, 'Thou
knowest it altogether.' It speaks of

Something incredibly possible

You see, the Good Book acknowledges that the tongue can
no *man* tame.

I think God is concerned about two areas. The first is, the
inconsistencies that dishonour the name of Christ. And that
brings us to the last pair of James' illustrations, a fountain
and a fruit tree. Somebody goes for a drink of water – and it
is foul water. Somebody hopes to find certain fruit – there is
no fruit. I think what James has in mind is the
disappointment that people experience with the incon-

sistency that dishonours the Lord. I sometimes wonder if there are more people today wanting to know about the right way, than we give credit to. I met a Roman Catholic lady recently at a charity supper. She knew what I was, because I had my dog-collar on; and we had not been talking very long before she turned to me and said: 'You know, I find faith very difficult.' For I suppose twenty minutes, we had a lovely talk about how faith comes by hearing and doing the Word of God. I wonder how many people we rub shoulders with want to know, and when they meet you they are so disappointed; they think they will get a draught of sweet water, but they do not; they think they will find something they ought to find in the life of a Christian, and they do not find it.

I remember G Harding Wood – 'Uncle Harding' – saying that once when he was a vicar in Hampstead, he was visiting the chauffeur at one of the big houses to discuss the baptism of a new baby, and when he had finished he asked if he could meet the man's employer. So it was arranged, and Uncle Harding chatted away for a while to this young man, who was so rich that he said to Uncle Harding that he didn't know how much money he possessed – and then Uncle Harding said, 'Do you mind if I ask you a question? Are you a Christian?'

The young man sat back and said, 'Why do you ask that?' And Uncle Harding said, 'Well, I'm a vicar, I suppose it's my job.' The young man said, 'I want to tell you something. I am not religious, I don't go to church and I don't pray. But not long ago I was in the North in a cathedral city and I had an overwhelming desire to pray. I went inside and knelt down; I don't know how long I prayed for, but while praying a voice seemed to say to me clearly, 'Go home at once, and I will send somebody to speak to you about Me.' That was three days ago, and I have been waiting.'

How many people are waiting? Waiting for you, for me, to say something? The inconsistency that dishonours the name of Christ. The impossibility that demands the grace of God.

My third heading is *Something incredibly possible*, because James does not say that the tongue cannot be tamed;

he says that man cannot do it. What we cannot do, He can. I wonder how? One verse holds the key, and it was spoken by Jesus Himself. Matthew 12:34, 'Out of the abundance of the heart the mouth speaketh.' What really fills our hearts will flow from our lips.

I knew a retired minister and his wife in Troon, and before I visited them I always knew what the conversation was going to be about. It would be all about their three grown-up sons. They were so full of them, they just could not talk about anything else! What was in their hearts came out of their lips. If I go to Liverpool and meet a class of boys, what will come out of their mouths? Talk of football. That is what fills their minds. And if Christ is really filling your life and mine, if the Holy Spirit is really allowed to do all that He wants to do in your life and mine, we really cannot keep it in. It is going to come out, it is going to control what we say.

Is this possibly one of the big areas of failure? There is an impossibility that demands the grace of God. I love that little phrase about Jesus, 'They wondered at the gracious words He spoke.' Do you speak graciously?

I remember being rebuked once in my fairly young days at Keswick. Dear Clarence Foster was the man who had the grace and goodness of God to rebuke me. Older folk will remember him, he was the Convention Secretary for many years. I don't know what I said – we were just making our way to a meeting, and I said something to him. He turned to me, and said, 'George, I am surprised. This is the first time I have ever heard you say an unkind word.'

'They wondered at the gracious words He spoke.'

So let us take that little phrase out of Psalm 139:4; may God grant that they may be gracious words, timely words that the Holy Spirit can use, for His glory.

DIVERSIONS AND ROAD BLOCKS

by Rev David Jackman

Hebrews 12:12-17

I wonder, have you had that frustrating experience of trying to get somewhere only to find it is impossible? Maybe you've been driving in a town you don't know, and all the one-way systems seem to be against you. Every way you turn it's 'Road blocked' or 'No entry' signs, or a diversion. You just can't seem to get where you want to be, and you travel round and round in circles until you're tempted to give up.

I think that sort of situation faces all of us at different stages of our Christian experience. We want to grow more like the Lord Jesus Christ; that's why He's saved us, to restore the image of God in His people; we want to know Him better, to love Him more. We want to serve Him more effectively and more consistently, and yet how often we are conscious of our failure. We are so frustrated by it that some of us begin to give up. We settle for the status quo, or we even begin to drift away. The writer of this very letter had to warn the Hebrews 'lest at any time we drift away' (2:1), as though all you have to do for that to happen is to tie up your boat with a loose knot, and the tide with its resistless power will do the rest.

I want to talk to you tonight about road blocks on the way to being the sort of Christian God wants you and me to be. As you know, this letter was written to Christians who were being tempted to give up. They were being persecuted for their faith in the Lord Jesus. If they were prepared to compromise a bit, to go back under the umbrella of Judaism, the external pressures would be lessened (though actually, there would be much greater internal pressures, for the Holy Spirit in a believer always begins to exert His pressure in a way that makes us realise what's happening). And so in this letter we have some marvellous teaching about the sufficiency of Jesus Christ, but with it some of the straightest warnings in the whole of the New Testament about compromise in our Christian lives and in our discipleship. Verses 14-16 of our passage focus the letter's teaching with great relevance for us today, because although we are at present unpersecuted we live in a society where the forces which are anti-Christ gain ground daily.

Look with me please at verse 14. Let me begin by asking you, what effort are you putting into your life as a Christian? What consumes your time, your energy, your talents? It's so easy, in our busy world, for our Christian faith to become a hobby to which we devote time in what we are pleased to call our 'spare time'. But here the writer speaks of harmony and holiness as essential ingredients of a life pleasing to God. Are these your priorities? It's interesting that the verb translated in the NIV as 'make every effort' is a verb that means 'run after' or 'pursue' – it was used for persecuting. These persecuted Christians were told to persecute something themselves, to seek harmony and holiness. The implication is that there should be a relentless, unwearied constant direction in our lives towards these priorities; a determination not to be blocked or diverted.

I ask myself, do we have a passion like that for holiness? The word has so often been devalued. We are not talking about some 'holier-than-thou' moral superiority. We are talking about being like the Lord Jesus. Do you have a passion to be like Christ? Are you making an effort? Do you want to see the Lord? For 'without holiness no-one will see the Lord'.

Now in the next two verses (15 and 16), the Holy Spirit highlights three areas in which, He teaches us, we are to examine ourselves severely. We are told to 'look carefully' in three areas: be careful no-one misses the grace of God; be careful no bitter root grows up; be careful no-one is sexually immoral or godless (again, the verb is interesting – it's unique in the New Testament and is used of a marksman aiming at his target). Says the writer, put your life under that sort of scrutiny. Look with the light that God shines from His Word on your way of life, and ask yourself: Where are these road blocks?

Firstly, let me suggest to you that in verse 15 there's *a failure to appropriate God's resources*. Here the failure is in the area of our relationship with God Himself. It is by grace we are saved. God in His mercy has opened our eyes to His truth as it is in the Lord Jesus. His Spirit has drawn us to Christ, we have found in Him the one who died that we might be forgiven, and we have experienced the forgiveness of our sins and then the implanting of God's Holy Spirit within us. We know something of the life of God within our own lives and personalities. And all that is God's grace, as the old acrostic definition says:

God's
Riches
At
Christ's
Expense

But – says the writer – you can fail to appropriate God's resources. Think of the wealth that is in the Lord Jesus. Think of the means by which it comes to us. It is by the grace of God that we are here at all; but it is equally only by the grace of God that we can continue in the Christian faith and complete the journey. God is committed to His people to provide grace to help in time of need. God's grace, rich and inexhaustible!

We can sin against that grace by failing to appropriate its resources. If that is so it is not because the supply of grace is exhausted. It is because we fail to appropriate that grace. We give way to what this writer has called (3:12) 'an evil heart of unbelief'. Put your life under the scrutiny of God's Word. Do we not sometimes behave as though the living God no longer existed? As though the reservoir had run dry and God were saying to us: Well, there is grace to save but not to keep or empower; you are on your own now?

We live like that sometimes. We say: Surely God can't be that gracious; surely we have to do our bit to earn it – and by that sin of unbelief we fail to appropriate the grace of God in Jesus Christ.

But you cannot be holy unless you draw on His resources. I want to ask you, is the road block in your life overconfidence in what you do? In some of our churches we have got God so sewn up that some areas of expansion and launching out in faith are no-go areas as far as we are concerned. It's so easy to fall back from grace into our evangelical works. We become increasingly dry. There is no forward movement without the grace of God, and that's why some of us are such static Christians, why we fall into the same sins again and again. Isn't it time there was a remake, that we began to appropriate the resources of grace that are constantly available?

Secondly, in verse 15, there is *a failure to appreciate God's purposes*. If the first area of failure is predominantly in the area of our relationship with God, here quite obviously it is in our relationships with each other in the Church. And this road block has widespread effects. The 'bitter root' in verse 15 takes us back to Deuteronomy 29:18,19, where Moses warns the Israelites against the danger of being influenced to idolatry by the Canaanites. The root of the problem is in 29:17: 'even though I persist in going my own way' – there is the road block, putting my purposes before God's and squeezing Him into the margin of my life, and then comforting myself by saying: I'm a Christian; so all will be well, God will overlook it.

But such self-indulgence has a ruinous effect on the whole community of God. It frustrates His purposes of harmony and holiness. 'Trouble' (verse 15) is the opposite of harmony, and 'defiled' is the opposite of holiness. There is a progression here. The unbelief in the first part of the verse leads to the idolatry of the second part.

Is that your road block? The gods of the nations – power,

success, security, wealth? Has your Christian experience, or perhaps your status as a Christian leader, or even your Christian service itself, taken over the place of God in your life and so become a road block? Or is it your own comfort, your security, your ambitions? The writer says here, this is a bitter root which will defile many.

Somebody recently said those classic words to me, 'I can forgive, but I cannot forget.' I said to her, 'Why do you say that? Are you not really saying, "My feelings are more important to me than God's grace?" Is the bitterness in your life a bitterness towards another Christian, whom perhaps you meet each Sunday – but there's an unforgiving spirit in you destroying your spiritual life?' Bitterness is a killer. 'See to it that no bitter root grows up.'

Maybe it's even bitterness against God. Why did He let that happen? Why was something for which I prayed not granted me? And the devil will see that we dwell upon it until God is gradually dethroned and it begins to take over. Others are affected; we begin to lose sight of God's purposes to build a harmonious, holy people and we become a poisonous herb in God's garden, always critical, censorious, touchy, hard, envious of others. That can be a road block not only to God's purposes being fulfilled in me, but in our Church and in His world. What an awesome thing that is!

Thirdly in verse 16, there is *a failure to apply God's standards to our lives*. Here the area of failure is our relationship to the world in which we live. It seems to me that the common denominator between the two very different parts of this verse is the desire for short-time gain at the expense of God's priorities. And that is always the essence of temptation. The unbelief that led to idolatry leads ultimately to behaviour that breaks God's law. I have met young Christians who tell me that they do not feel convicted about sleeping together although they are unmarried, and that because they don't feel it, surely it must be all right, and that God is blessing them because they have no feeling in their hearts that they are wrong. But God's Word is utterly against fornication, as it is against the lust of the eyes from which fornication springs. We cannot live a holy life and also infringe God's laws, for the law is the expression of the holy character of God. God's law is not simply a collection of the arbitrary restrictions. It expresses the nature of the God who reveals Himself through that law. And when He says that the law governing sexual relationships is faithfulness within marriage and no sexual relationships outside it, that is an expression of the faithful character of God and His commitment to His people in covenant blessing. When the Scripture says, 'Run from immorality', it reflects the character of the holy God who calls us to holiness. Therefore, if we mean business in the Christian life we must apply His standards to what we watch, what we read, what we say. How much we in our society need enthusiasm for purity before God, for singleness of heart and mind in His presence, for holiness. How much we need to pray that God will grant us that down-to-earth reality of His Spirit, granting us that holiness in practice, so we don't snatch what God has ordained for marriage from that context of mutual responsibility and love.

And what of Esau, the archetypal materialist, in verse 16? His godlessness is what is singled out. So little did he value his God-given birthright, that he was prepared to give it up for the most immediate trivial satisfaction of his appetite. Be careful, says the writer, that you are not like Esau.

How can I be like him? Well, by putting my own material well-being before the will of God. You see, it comes back to a very practical question: Are my material resources really at God's disposal? Are my talents His? My time, energy, money, home? Who controls it all? Are my resources, that He's first given me, back in His hands at His disposal? Or is my attitude: Well, they're my resources and any left-overs can be God's? If that's the way we're thinking, it is a road block.

How tragic to be an Esau, consumed by remorse (as verse 17 shows him), unable to undo the consequences of his sin, because he would not apply the standards of God to his life. And, while we can thank God that verse 24 points us to Jesus, the Mediator of a new covenant and to the sprinkled blood that speaks a better word than the blood of Abel – let us never forget that though there is a cleansing from sin, a forgiveness and restoration with the Lord, yet it remains true that we may have to live with the consequences of our sin, just as Esau had to live with the consequences of his failure to apply God's standards. God can restore wonderfully, but there are many who are today living with the consequences of situations and decisions they took in the past, which have led them step by step further away from God. And though He has brought them back to Himself, sin sometimes has long-lasting effects in our relationships and lives. That is why the Scripture warns us so strongly against it. That is why this little passage says to us, 'Make every effort to live in peace with all men, and to be holy.'

That is why I believe God is saying to us, 'Have you been building road blocks in your life? Are there any no-go areas in your life as far as God is concerned? Are you living on your spiritual capital and resources, or are you daily appropriating His grace at every point of need? Are you directed by your will, or are God's purposes of a harmonious and holy fellowship what motivate you and make you say, "I want to be the best for God, in this day of opportunity He has given us"?'

That is the message He is bringing us in this passage. What are we really living for? Do we want to be like the Lord Jesus? That is holiness, without which no-one will see the Lord. And while that holiness is entirely of God's grace, this verse will teach us that it is also dependant upon making every effort. We have to co-operate with that grace. We have to respond to it. We have to receive it, and not to miss it.

UZZIAH THE KING

by Dr Raymond Brown

*This address was given immediately after that given
by Rev David Jackman (p.132).*

2 CHRONICLES 26

The story of King Uzziah is a familiar one. He made a
magnificent beginning in his life as a man of God, but he
came to a desperately tragic end.

It's a very tragic story. And it must have something to say
to us; there's no doubt about that. Old Testament stories are
not just there to enrich our understanding of the history of
the people of Israel. They do that, but they have a greater
purpose. You will remember that when the Apostle Paul
wrote his letter to the Romans, he said that the 'things that
happened aforetime' were written for our learning as
Christians, that we through the encouragement of the
Scriptures might have hope. When he wrote to that very
mixed and rather troubled and sinful church at Corinth, he
said that the things that had happened from the time of
Exodus were to be as an example to us. The Old Testament is
a lesson book for a believer.

So, though the times are very different, and though –
thank God – resources in Christ are so much greater, these
stories have something very powerful to say to us about our
own lives.

This, then, is the story of a man who made a brilliant
beginning but came to a tragic end. It didn't happen
suddenly. It happened quite gradually. And there must be
something here for us, because Uzziah isn't alone in that.
There are many stories in the Bible of people who started off

wonderfully, with all the resources of God at their disposal, with so much promise. Other people would have been blessed and enriched by their dedication and their zeal. But instead there were road blocks in their lives. They didn't fulfil the purposes of God in holiness and harmony. They came to a desperately unhappy end themselves, and wrought havoc in the lives of others,

Gideon made a wonderful beginning – he felt himself to be a coward, yet he was given great power. The spirit of humility and dependence came upon him, and he wrought wonderful things for God. And yet, he became greedy. When they offered him the place of kingship, he said: 'No! I don't want to be a king. The Lord's going to rule over you. But . . . if you *have* got a little bit of gold . . . a few gold earrings . . . I've got a nice robe here, I'm spreading it on the ground. You can show your appreciation, not by putting a crown on my head, but by slipping some rings on to this robe on the floor.' And he made an ephod with it. It says in the Book of Judges that not only was it a grief to Gideon, but a stumbling block to the people of Israel.

Young Saul made a marvellous beginning; he said almost the same words as Gideon had. 'I'm not fit for the role of king . . . you've got the wrong man here, I'm not fitted for this work at all!' There was a spirit of humility and dependence upon him. And yet, he went wrong, he became greedy too. He did that which was not lawful. In a moment of impatience he offered sacrifice. It wasn't his role to do that. By and by his life was spoilt and ruined so that at the end he said 'I have played the fool.'

And it goes on, into the New Testament. Judas began just like the rest, he heard the same matchless preaching, looked into the same lovely eyes, saw the same beautiful example as the other eleven. But greed crept in, and instead of the love of Christ he chose a handful of coins. And they hadn't been in his hands for hours before he saw how cheap and worthless they were.

Go on into the period of the New Testament Church, to the letter to the Colossians, where Paul is delighting in the companionship of a young man called Demas, who was loyal and good and true. But writing to young Timothy, at the end of his days, Paul says, 'Demas has forsaken me, having loved this present world.'

And here is the story of an Old Testament king who began with wonderful promise, and reigned for over half a century. In his teens he was someone who determined to live beautifully for God. But the story goes on to say that he became strong and that when he became strong he became self-reliant and self-dependent. Life became so successful and prosperous for him, nothing could go wrong. And he was living without God. He was living on the externals.

And then, he became false to the Lord. It started with self-reliance, and it moved to self-exaltation; and then it went on to self-destruction. I want you to think about him at the beginning, and maybe have the courage in the presence of God and by the ministry of the Holy Spirit to reflect on our own beginnings. Have we grown and developed in holiness? Or do we look back wistfully – 'Where is the blessedness I knew, when first I sought the Lord . . .'

Oh, Uzziah made a marvellous beginning. He was a disciplined man: verse 5, he 'set himself'. He did what was right in the eyes of the Lord – he was concerned only for His honour and glory. He knew all too well the stories of earlier kings who had started well, with love for God and loyalty to His truth, but had failed miserably; he wasn't going to be like that, so he determined, set himself, to seek the Lord. He drew deep on those springs of endless resources that God has for any believing man or woman who seeks Him in prayer.

He was not only disciplined, he was gifted; because he came to God in prayer God poured into his life wonderful qualities. If you read the passage it is almost embarrassing to see how this man crowds into one life a number of achievements, any one of which would have satisfied any man on its own. He possessed military, architectural, and agricultural skills. He was a marvellous administrator, with great organising ability (verse 11). He recognised the qualities of engineers (verse 15). He had international fame. 'His fame spread far, for he was marvellously helped . . .

Till he was strong.'

My friends, there's nothing so dangerous as success. If you feel you have failed you may well be driven to the place where you see your need – but beware of success. Beware of being carried on by achievement. If God has blessed you, that's wonderful! – as long as it keeps you in the holy place. As long as you pray as earnestly as you did before the success came. The awful, terrifying danger with each one of us is, that when we have any kind of success we are not quite so dependent on the Lord as we were when our backs were against the wall, when we knew that without His help we would utterly fail, when we were drawing on those resources because we had none of our own. There was no-one else to whom we could go.

But you see, when you prosper, when your particular form of Christian work just bristles with encouragement, when you're swimming along in your Christian life, there's a sense of buoyancy that keeps you up, and gradually and imperceptibly that sense of dependence on God can quietly drain away. You hardly know it. You won't notice it for a week or two; maybe not even for a month or two. But gradually, you will be praying less and working more. You will be reading less of the Word, but perhaps listening more – going to more and more meetings, packing your life with activity of one kind and another. But in all the noise and busy-ness, the sense of utter dependence upon the Lord is seeping away.

What were Uzziah's faults? How did the self-reliance come to be? What are his mistakes? Well, they are clearly outlined for us in the passage. It's an Old Testament lesson-book for us. I want to suggest one or two of his failings to you, because they may find a sad echo in the hearts of some of us.

Is it possible that Uzziah was one of those people who relied far too much on the supportive help of other people, and not enough on the Lord Himself? Notice verse 5. As long as he sought the Lord, God made him prosper. Zechariah was his teacher, and while he was receiving this instruction he leaned on him, but Zechariah disappears from the scene. You read about all the marvellous achievements (verses 6-15), but no mention of Zechariah. Maybe Zechariah was his teacher early on in his believing experience, when he first came to the throne and was driven into the presence of God; and Zechariah said to him day after day, as he taught him the things of God and especially taught him about the holiness of God: 'Young Uzziah, don't slip away from God.'

He relied on this man, depended upon him. Isn't it easy for this to happen to you? You don't have to pursue only bad things – you can find yourself depending on good things, but not on God Himself. How many people are there in fine keen churches, for example, who contribute wonderfully to the life of a live congregation, and then they move to another part of the country. You try to link them up with the minister. They are different people when they get away from that congregation. Oh! they were all right when there were hundreds around them, but they go to another district, with a smaller church, and it doesn't match the pattern they knew before, and they gradually slip away. They were actually kept going by the faith of other people. It was the sense of buoyancy they felt in a big congregation. There was nothing spiritual about it. It was a huge psychological, even sensual thing. God was still in the district to which they moved; the Lord was there; there was still work for them to do. But they were only all right when they were being taught in the way they felt they wanted. Like Uzziah; he was all right when Zechariah was boosting him, leading him along. But he drew away, after that.

There's a second failure, mentioned with clarity in the passage. Uzziah came to carelessly neglect the privilege of prayer. Verse 5: 'As long as he sought the Lord, God made him prosper.' The implication is that there came a day when he didn't seek the Lord, he just relied on the prosperity. And prayer slipped out of his life. Oh, I don't doubt he went through all the religious ceremonial expected of a king. But he didn't seek God's face.

When you don't pray, you have really made yourself a practical atheist. You may believe in God in the 'top level' of your mind, but not in the bottom of your heart. If you don't pray you're really saying to God, 'I can do without you.' Only by praying are we expressing our dependence and confidence. They need not be spoken or formal prayers, but if we lift our hearts to God and beg that He will fill us with His Spirit, His resources, His grace – then we shall be all right.

Here's the third failure. You would have thought, with his achievements, qualities, virtues and gifts, that he had enough to satisfy anyone. And yet, he still looked covetously at something else. He was a man who looked covetously at the achievements of others. One day – it was pure formality, he'd drifted away from God – he was present in the Temple. He saw the priests officiating. And he thought, 'I'm a good soldier, a capable organiser, a gifted engineer, a keen agriculturist. I'd quite like to be a priest.'

The work of a priest was reserved for the appropriate tribe, to maintain God's holiness and sanctity. But he'd wandered away from God, he hadn't listened to His law. He didn't think for one moment about the holiness of God that he'd learned from Zechariah years before. He said. 'I'm as good as they are any day. I'm not thinking about what God has said in the past – I'm worried about what they think of me in the present.' He just walked forward, snatched the censer and started officiating as a priest. The priests were horrified, and told him he was doing something which was grieving God. Instead of being content with all he had got, he was lusting for more. It was Adam's sin at the beginning, wasn't it? Not listening to what God says is appropriate, what's right and what's wrong.

The priest warns him he ought to go out of the sanctuary, but instead of responding in meekness and repentance he becomes angry. That moment when he heard that warning was the most dramatic moment of his life. It was then that he faced his greatest crisis. If at that moment he had just dropped the censer and said 'Sorry', he could have been a pardoned man. But he became angry. And when he became angry – not when he grasped the censer, but when became angry – when he couldn't take correction, then the leprosy rose in his forehead.

Perhaps the most dangerous moment is not when you sin,

although that's awful enough, and no-one wants to underestimate it. But it's a far more dangerous moment when you become aware you've done wrong, but you don't do anything about it. You go on persisting in sin. The awful thing about Uzziah was that he lost his sense of the holiness of God, and he objected to the correcting ministry that was extended to him.

He became a leper to the day of his death. A terribly sad story, of a man who reached a point when he ought to have known that he had sinned, and could easily have said he was sorry, but instead reacted in bitterness and wrath.

Maybe in this study we have become aware of things in our lives that are not what they ought to be. The searchlight of God's Spirit has shone deep into our hearts; the plough share has gone deep into our minds, and there's an opportunity now to put it right. We can go out forgiven – or resentful.

I don't want you to leave, thinking of this sad man with his desperately disfigured face; with his marvellous beginning and tragic ending. You are to think about a different face, at exactly the same time in Hebrew history. It's the face of a young man who goes into that Temple to pray, and in the year that King Uzziah died, he sees the Lord (Isaiah 6:1). He realises he is in the presence of a holy God; the cherubim call to one another, 'Holy, holy, holy is the Lord of Hosts,' and the young Isaiah takes upon his lips which he says are unclean, this word not of arrogance but of confession: 'Woe is me, I'm lost; I am a man of unclean lips.' Unclean – that's the leper's word. Had he learned this from this tragic experience of this sad and tragic king?

Then one of the cherubim comes to him with live coals from the altar. 'Your sin, your iniquities are taken away, and your sin is purged.'

Oh, what a different ending! A man who is aware of his need, but doesn't respond in anger and resentment, who takes the correction of God's Spirit; and He drives him to that place where pardon is not only offered, but available.

My prayer for you, as it is for me, is that we will make our confession and not respond to this evening's ministry in any sense of bitterness or resentment, but with gratitude. Because it's only those who are loved who are corrected. Be zealous therefore; and repent.

UNCOMFORTABLE WORDS

by Rev Dick Lucas

Matthew 11:25-30

He who understands the words that we are going to study tonight has found his way to the heart of Christianity, so it ought to be worthwhile to study them. We turn then to the most wonderful words, probably, ever spoken by the Lord Jesus Christ. Here we have the heart of Christianity brought to your heart and mine.

The wonderful words of verse 28 are inscribed in the old Church of England prayer book, under the title 'comfortable words'. I'm not sure that the title is a good one; it gives the impression that when Jesus spoke it was like a healing ointment applied to a scratch on a finger, as though the words of Christ were a perpetual outflow of ointment to calm us all down and comfort us and make life very easy. When I was young you didn't have many of these ointments, you used to go to the chemist and buy iodine. And one's mother would plonk that on one's scar or scratch; and wow! did it hurt, did it sting!

Very often when I read the words of the Lord Jesus it's not like ointment, it's like iodine; and this passage has got a good deal of iodine in it. There are some very *un*-comfortable words. And I want to bring you three uncomfortable words in this famous passage, words that you know very well; and yet I wonder whether you realise how they sting? And let me say this; when I talk about stinging, I mean a sting like when you go out on a really cold morning when there's a severe frost. It almost catches you by the throat – yet it's wonderfully bracing, isn't it? The teaching of Jesus is like that frosty morning, when I catch it in the throat and I realise that this is the air to breathe.

Now in this passage, Jesus stands in judgement on certain things, and two things in particular.

Jesus stands in judgement on the wisdom of the world

He speaks of the total failure of human wisdom to solve the problems of the world. His words are provocative to a degree. Just imagine Him standing in front of the crowd, they're waiting for Him to start – and He looks up to heaven and says, 'Lord I thank You so much, My Father, that You've hidden all these things from the wise and understanding, and You've revealed them to babies.'

I wonder what they made of it? I hasten to say, He's not saying: 'Before you can come to this meeting, leave your brains outside.' No, what He's talking about is something that was very common then and is very common today – those who listen, but are wise in their own hearts. He is saying, 'Father, I thank You that You have hidden all these things from anybody who's wise in his own mind and knows all the answers.' And that means most of us in the twentieth century. Jesus says, if you are like that, if you are a child of your age, you will remain baffled.

For nearly a hundred years in the western world there has been immense pride. Pride in scientific method, in education, in the inevitability of progress; pride in our human skill to conquer the obvious barriers on the way to happiness. But I'm glad to be alive as we come towards the end of the twentieth century, because there is disillusionment, not least amongst young people. Indeed, we have all realised that these vaunted claims have not made it a happier world. There are many today who despair of human progress and wonder whether it's all going to end in some colossal bang, some terrible catastrophe – because there are so many fools on the political and diplomatic field today, aren't there?

And yet it's amazing how long this lie has continued. The twentieth century! The century of progress! We've put aside all these superstitions, all this old Christian faith . . . we'll go into the *Brave New World*! Well, I don't think anybody honestly thinks that now, and if they do, I'd like to shake them.

I spent a remarkable week of mission some years ago in a school. I was given permission to speak to the schoolchildren in the school hall each day at four o'clock, and a large number of schoolchildren from the various schools came together for a talk and question time. You know the sort of thing that happens in a question time like that – hands shoot up everywhere and you get this kind of cheeky question from teenagers: 'Well, Sir, if you can explain why God made such a bad job of the world, I might believe. Can you tell me the meaning of these things?'

Poor old God, there in the dock, He's got to give an explanation of Himself to this teenager. The teenager has said he will believe if God will be pleased to give the answers. Is that really the situation? Isn't it actually that we have got to give an explanation of ourselves to God, of the mess we've made of the world and of our lives, even with all this knowledge and education?

Well, as I was speaking at that mission one evening, we'd been going for about half an hour and then some young people were brought in from a spastics' grammar school nearby. Some of them were unable to speak at all or to move their limbs with regularity. Afterwards I went to talk to them, and I found that they were razor-sharp in their minds; and I found in them an amazing humility. They asked me to go to their school, and I went the next afternoon and found the attitude was very different from the other schools. Not: 'If God could possibly give me an answer – but of course He can't – I might believe'; not that kind of nonsense, but 'I don't know why I'm in this position, but I do want to know what you've come to say, I do want to hear what God has to say.' I couldn't believe it; we had a wonderful hour.

I've thought about that ever since, and I think possibly the reason for it is that if you are dependent on other people even to carry you into the bathroom, if you're dependent on others all your life, it teaches you a certain humility.

Now what did Jesus say? 'Babies' – those who are dependent on others. That's all it means. He is using a vivid picture of those willing to ask questions because they don't know. I thank God that I live in a world where people are returning and saying 'We do not know: all the promised solutions that were paraded before us are not there; perhaps we'd better go back to God and ask Him, "Is there an answer? Will You tell us? Because we don't know."' The first mark of sanity returning is – 'I don't know, I have failed.'

Christ stands in judgement on human wisdom. And I thank God that many people are sitting in judgement on it too, and they're beginning to seek in earnest. That's why so many young people are turning to religion, all sorts of quaint religions. Maybe, if science hasn't got the answer, religion has?

Well, no; indeed science has not got the answer. God has laughed and had us in derision, hasn't He? He has allowed us to go our own way, and he has been proved right, the result has not been happy.

Jesus stands in judgement on the religion of the world

Jesus does not only judge the wisdom of the world. He stands in judgement, in these remarkable verses, on its religion. What is happening today is that many people, thoughtful people, are turning in the direction of religion. They don't know where to turn to, and many religions are advertising their wares on many walls. But people are turning in that direction because they say human progress has not worked, and perhaps religion will.

Perhaps it is a shock to find that Jesus stands in judgement on religion. You may say, how do I prove that? Well, look at verse 28. You will never understand that sentence of Jesus unless you look at Matthew 23:3, 4. That is iodine; it stings. Now for myself, though I think the 'burden' of Matthew 11:28 includes the burden of sin, I think it is also the burden that religious people have laid. He's talking to the world. 'You've showed, you've sought, you've gone on a long weary journey to find the truth and you've never found it. And when you've gone to religion, what has religion done for you? It's laid these burdens upon you.'

I remember my own preparation for Confirmation. What burdens were laid upon me; no good news, nothing about Christ. I was led along the pathway of sincere devoted religion. I can only say, it failed me and the other forty boys. We were looking for a miracle; obviously miracles weren't around, today.

Think of the television programmes on religion. How futile they are, aren't they? *The Long Search* – the long search indeed. When I open the Bible I don't find the sheep is having a long search for the shepherd. Imagine it finding its way back at the right time and place. Who's doing the searching in the New Testament? Not man, not the philosopher, the twentieth-century enquirer, the television programme, nine grand programmes ending in cliché and waffle. It's God who's doing the searching in the New Testament. It's the Shepherd looking for the sheep. Yes; there is a long search. And the one who instituted it is God.

And what do I put in His way, lest He should come too close to me? Why, I often put religion; man is very good at that. What has made many of the countries of the world what they are? Their religion. And often it's been a heavy burden.

Now what has He set over against religion? I think this is the most breathtaking thing in all our Lord's teaching. Read verse 27. Read it with awe. 'Come to me' – not 'Go to the scribes and Pharisees, go to religion like so many of your countrymen.' 'Come to Me'! Staggering, isn't it! Look at the sweeping language: 'all ... no-one ... any one ... all things ...' And who will come to Him? Just those whom He chooses. If you go the way of religion, there will be burden; and if you come His way, 'I will give you rest.'

Archbishop William Temple said that Christianity is not a religion, it's a revelation. That is exactly what is said here. 'Anyone to whom the Son chooses to reveal Him.' How I thank God that Christ, in a sense, redeemed me from religion! I'd had some good religious experiences, but it never saved my soul. It never brought me into direct contact with God so I could pray to Him and love Him. Thank God I was saved from 'being religious' to find God: it's quite different, isn't it? We are saved to be human beings, to be the men or women God meant us to be, not to be religious, not to be a curious kind of specimen; but to be a full human being, reconciled to God. 'Come unto Me, all who are heavy laden' – all who've looked for the truth, all you who've been to church all your life and never found it, all who are laden with the burden of guilt, of failure, of atheism, of agnosticism. 'Come to Me ... and I will give you rest.'

Now on these things, Christ stands in judgement. He does so today. He stands in judgement on the wisdom of the world. It cannot lead to life as God plans it. Only God can reveal to us His purposes; he will do so only through Jesus Christ. Jesus stands here in judgement on all religion that does not have Him at the centre. The great thing – a really shocking thing – about the New Testament is that everything is centred on the letter 'I'. We don't talk, do we, about religion or ceremonies so much, as Christ? If you're a Christian, that is what's precious, isn't it? That is what is on your lips. To know Christ, to love Him, enjoy Him forever ... can you believe it?

I want to say as we finish that though in this passage He does not do so openly, by implication Christ stands in judgement on one more thing.

Jesus stands in judgement on superficial Christian discipleship

The world's problems won't be solved, either, by superficial Christian discipleship. Look very carefully at verses 28 and 29. I would say at once that I don't believe that it is meant to describe two different kinds of Christians – but I'm afraid it often does.

To come to Jesus, in the biblical vocabulary, is to take His yoke upon you. Those two things mean the same. But we're forced to say that though that is theologically correct it is not what we observe. We hear wonderful things from the USA, we see new things in our own country, we hear of so many in America calling themselves 'born again Christians' – but we hear other voices saying, 'Is this making any difference to our world? Is it going to change things?' It's all very well to be a new man – but if it doesn't lead to a new world, what's happening?

And so I just want to tie these up in our experience. I've found it very moving to realise that verses 28 and 29 are held together and are meant never to be divorced. I remember meeting an Archbishop of the Ukrainian Church in New York. He as a youngster had attended a Methodist Sunday school. I asked him why he'd left the Methodists. He said, 'Well, I went every Sunday for three years. Each Sunday, the lesson was the same; "You must be born again." I began after a while to think that there must be more to Christianity than that.' There are churches, aren't there, assemblies, companies of Christian people, who meet every Sunday to preach verse 28, full stop. We've all heard it a thousand times. We never go any further.

Well, we do; surely, I hope we do, I hope I'm caricaturing. Because surely we must go on to verse 29. 'Take My yoke upon you' – we must accept not only the gift of His rest but also the gift of His rule. That is what the word means; the yoke of somebody who rules; not a foreign oppressor, but the Lord of glory.

Now very simply and practically I want to tell you what it will mean to take that yoke if you've never seriously done so before. I speak now to you who are Christians. And I ask you seriously: you have taken His yoke of lordship upon you. But has it been practical? Has it been worked-out?

It means three things. It means, to *submit to study*. 'Learn of Me.' I'm praying at Keswick, for people who will take on their shoulders the yoke of Christ, to become students of His school; who will start serious Bible study, to study it so seriously that they do it and then go on to teach it. Like Ezra – to study, to do and to teach.

Will you take the yoke of Christ to be a student at His feet, to study as seriously as you study for anything else in this world? Will you say, Lord, teach me to pray, teach me to teach others? Will you take the yoke on your shoulders, to be a student who may one day teach others? You'll have to learn a lot if you're going to teach others.

Secondly, there is *the yoke of submission*. 'Take My yoke upon you and learn from Me; for I am gentle and lowly in heart.' Lord Jesus – did You *really* say that? You're the Lord of the universe! Well, then, if I'm going to walk with You, I've got to be the same. We can't disagree about the way we walk. Amazing, isn't it, how God leads us. God will ask many of you to humble yourselves. It's actually not something you only do once. You've got to go on doing it all your life, to humble yourself in the mighty hand of God. It's quite a good idea, in fact, to try to do one thing a day that humbles you. It hurts a lot, doesn't it, when we're humiliated? We can learn to do it daily. It's awfully good for us. It's sometimes very painful; and sometimes these things are done for us, without our doing them. But I must say I wish I'd known, right at the beginning of my Christian life, that if I wanted to prance along cockily and proudly and be yoked also to Jesus Christ who is lowly and humble of heart, I was going to find it a very rough ride.

He's going to make you a servant whether you like it or not, Christian person, and He'll have to chasten you. 'Lord, this yoke is so painful!' 'Yes, it's very painful – because your neck is so stiff.'

How I long to be gentle and lowly – don't you? Well, I've got to take that yoke, it's going to hurt. Will you allow God to teach you that?

He's going to do it anyway. It just hurts more if you resist, that's all.

Lastly, *the yoke of service*. If you take the yoke of service, it will seem a burden. For example; to commit yourself regularly to Christian service every Sunday afternoon is a burden, because we like our Sundays rather freer, don't we? I have a lady who has done the lunches at our Tuesday mid-day services at St Helens for seventeen years, every Tuesday except holiday time. It must have been a burden sometimes, mustn't it. I think if she were here she would say verse 30 is true. 'My burden is light.'

I've said that this is part and parcel of ordinary Christianity. And yet I feel, just from observation of other people's lives and my own heart, that it's all too possible to rejoice in verse 28 and not to take verse 29 seriously. And I think Jesus stands in judgement on superficial Christian discipleship in the West, and that's not going to solve our problems either in the Church or in the world.

So I want to bring you the immense power of those words, and I want to bring this to your heart and conscience. In the name of Jesus, I want to say to you, take His yoke upon you and learn from Him. The yoke of study; the yoke of submission, in the family just as much as in the church; the yoke of service. Will you ask God to show you, before you go to sleep tonight, how that yoke is going to fit, and will you bend your proud neck if it's stiff? And I'll do the same.

And let's get up tomorrow morning rejoicing that the yoke is easy and the burden light.

'AND DAVID FOUND STRENGTH IN THE LORD HIS GOD'

by Rev Keith Weston

1 Samuel 30:6

I want to take tonight the end of 1 Samuel 30:6, which the New International Version translates, 'David found strength in the Lord his God.'

What we have been praying for as we have looked forward to this week in Keswick, I'm sure, is not so much a week of fellowship and holiday (though we trust it will be that); but that in some sense it may be a real turning point, a milestone, in our spiritual lives. May that be so! And, I'm sure we are praying also, may God do something to us here which will be also a turning point in our church fellowship, our country, our society. Yes, pray that this Convention could mark a turning point.

That is what really brings one, I think, to 1 Samuel 30, because I believe that in this verse you do in fact stand at the very eve of a marvellous turning point in the history of Israel; for the enigmatic reign of Saul is about to end. You read of his death in the next chapter.

And in some sense the golden age of Israel's reign is about to begin; but you don't see that here in 1 Samuel 30, because what we see there is a man in all his need. And it only becomes apparent as you read around this chapter and on into the next book that also what we see is a God in control. So there I have given you the two basic, very simple headings of our talk, and I trust that that will help you to see the way that we are going.

A man in need

Here we see a man in need – but look closer; for here we see a God who is in control. And it was to that God that David came and in that God found strength for all the future. And oh, pray God that this Convention might be a meeting with the God of history, the God who is in control; and that as we meet with Him we may find strength or encouragement for all that lies ahead for us.

A man in need. Now this chapter contains references which touch the nerve and answer to our need in our situation. Let me try and touch some of them for you.

The context is, first, one of tragedy. Ziklag was David's home at that time; and while David and his men had been away, the marauding Amelekites had come and they had raided the city. And when David returned, all he found was rubble and the smouldering embers of what remained, and worst of all, everything lost – loved ones, wives, sons, daughters missing; and they searched the ruins and they found none of them.

As I read verse 4, or verse 6, a context of tragedy and utter distress overtook them. The New English Bible translates verse 6, 'David was in a desperate position.' And there is a familiar ring about those words, isn't there, for us? What is happening in our society, when our cities are burned and attacked by marauding bands? Did you hear the reference to loot? Strangely up to date, isn't it? I am sure there is not one of us who is not deeply distressed by the events of these past months in our beloved country, and who knows, this Keswick Convention may have come at one of the most crucial points in our social history. Who knows? David did not realise it, in 1 Samuel 30, that this was to be a turning point in the history of Israel. For while he was bemoaning the ruins of his city, God was in action opening the way for the future.

It's a context, then, of tragedy. Aren't we all anxious? And we come to Keswick this year, perhaps, as we've never come before – deeply, right deep down in our hearts, disturbed. We are all asking, what is going on?

It's a context, secondly, of weariness. Through almost every chapter of First Samuel, David has been hounded from pillar to post. And this experience of coming back to Ziklag and finding it fired and looted must have been almost the last straw. 'They wept until they were completely exhausted' – as the Good News Bible translates verse 4. Read the psalms which accompany these chapters of First Samuel, and you will see the kind of thing it meant to David and no doubt to many other godly people in those days. 'Save me, O God,' he cries in Psalm 30; 'vindicate me, hear my prayer, for insolent men have risen against me, ruthless men seek my life.' That was when the Ziphites betrayed him. Or when he was hiding in some deserted cave away from Saul and his hungry hunting for David. 'Be merciful to me O God, be merciful,' he cries, 'they have set a net for my steps, my soul is bowed down.' He feels the burden of the situation that's upon him. 'I lie,' he says in Psalm 57, 'in the midst of lions that greedily devour the sons of men.'

And sometimes, brothers and sisters, it is hard, isn't it, to be a Christian? Maybe some of us have come to Keswick weary in some ways of the Christian pilgrimage, utterly exhausted in the battle against sin, the world and the devil. For some of us the circumstances of our Christian lives may have been particularly hard, and frankly, we are tired. We need strengthening, and maybe we have come with that at the forefront of our minds – 'God; I need refreshing . . .' 'And David found strength in the Lord his God.'

Look at the utter exhaustion of some of the people in this chapter. David sets out to try to recover all that's been lost, and indeed he succeeds; but they come to the brook Besor (verses 9 and 10). 200 of the 600 are too exhausted to go any further. 'I can't go on,' say 200 of them. One third of David's loyal men sink to the ground at Besor. 'I can't go on.' Utter weariness. Is that your context too? Some Christian minister who is finding his life in the ministry hard and perplexing. Some overseas missionary who's had a very hard last stint abroad – you're even wondering whether you ought to go back at all – you're weary. You're frankly physically tired, emotionally drained and spiritually weary. Or some parent;

parents are under pressure these days. Many of us rejoice to come here with our families, but you come with family responsibilities heavy on your shoulders. You're worried about your children. Maybe you're crying out to God over children who are not following in the Way, and you come weary and you need strengthening.

I believe this to be tremendously common. In one way or other most of us, I would guess, are people who need to find new strength in the Lord our God, and I believe that this is where we are going to find it; through the written word via the spoken word, to the living Word, who is Christ, who satisfies all our needs. You come and I come, simply aware of our needs. And the Lord is here, and His will and desire is to meet those needs whatever they may be, in one way or another, to make this Convention a turning point as we seek the Lord to find strength in Him.

In verse 6 we find *a context of criticism*. This rings bells for me and I suspect for many of us here, especially those in the ministry. Why did the people speak of stoning David? Because they wanted to blame him for the tragedy that had caught up with them. Can you hear their angry cries? Can you hear the bitterness in those verses as people hunted for their wives and children and none of them were there? Just smouldering ruins. And they all began to say, 'David's to blame.' And they began even to talk of putting him to death, of stoning him.

And such bitterness has a habit of spreading, even in a church, and verse 21 speaks of the folk coming back to these exhausted 200 by the brook Besor; and the 'wicked and mean and base fellows', it says, among the men of David, are critical and judgemental as they join their fellows. Criticism can be one of the hardest things to bear, especially when it's unjust and undeserved; and how battered and bruised some Christians can be because of what others say or do to them; and how deep are the scars some bear through the cruel criticism of others, even in the church fellowship, to whom they might have looked for encouragement. And I'm quite sure there may be some here this evening who know what I'm talking about. And ... David found strength in the Lord his

God. Isn't that beautiful?

It was, fourthly, a context of compromise; and here we're nearer the bone for some of us. It may not just be the outward circumstances which make people in need. David has much to answer for; for, as I read these verses there is an immediate background of compromise which should never have taken place. For sixteen months, you will see in 27:7, David has been dwelling, not only in the country of, but with the Philistines.

He said, in 27:1, 'I shall now perish one day by the hand of Saul.' Now, who told him that? All the indications were the opposite. God had a great plan for his life, greater than he could ever have dreamed of. But he was so dejected that he could say, 'Surely it's going to happen; I'm going to die at the hands of Saul. He's going to catch up with me after all one day. My luck won't hold, I'm finished. So there's nothing better to do but to escape to the Philistines.'

To the Philistines? David, what are you doing?

I don't know that he knew himself. I don't know that he argued it out. But it was to produce the most dreadful problem for him. True, for a time the pressure eased and Saul gave up chasing him there, but it was compromise and compromise always leads to cover-up and lies. Read these chapters, and see how David tells lie after lie there, until Achish the king feels that he has won David over completely, that David is now his servant for ever. All who compromise are heading for tragedy; and in these days I believe many of us need to learn this lesson again. Perhaps some of us are being led by the nose away from a clear-cut Christian profession into something which is conforming us to the world's standards. We are called as Christians not to be conformed, but to be transformed by the renewing of our minds. If we compromise with the flesh, we are compromising with the devil.

And what is David doing, marching with the lords of the Philistines? (29:1,2). Which side of the battle ought David to have been on? David, what are you doing there, passing on in the rear with Achish? Even the Philistine commanders spotted him. Sometimes the people of this world can be more acutely aware of that compromise even than Christians can be. And oh, that it should come from a pagan Philistine: 'What are these Hebrews doing here?'

In these difficult days, the battle lines are drawn up. Are you on the Lord's side – or are you not? Where are you? If you're on the wrong side, what are you doing there?

And all this is in the very chapter previous to the one we're studying . . . A context of compromise. Compromise is never, ever, the way to peace and joy in serving the Lord. Can it be that one of the things the Lord is going to do to us is to put His finger on some compromise we're hiding away, and say to us, 'What are you doing here?' What indeed was David doing there? We read that the Philistines were drawing up their battle lines against Israel, for the last fateful battle of Saul and Jonathan and the other sons of Saul. But in the mercy of God, David – who is marching on the wrong side – is prevented from going into battle against his fellow-countrymen.

What thoughts can have been in David's mind as he came to Ziklag and found it destroyed? Was there perhaps some ground of complaint on the part of those who blamed him and wanted him killed on the spot? I simply cannot believe that a heart like David's did not hide deep anxieties about his past behaviour. And who of us is without sin? Maybe in the pressures of life we've allowed compromise to creep in, we're on the wrong side, in some sense a defeated Christian; perhaps utterly prayerless, and we know it. Powerless in the Lord's ministry, and we desperately need to meet with the Lord our God.

I wish I could paint the scene, of David at Ziklag; the smouldering ruins around him and the murmurings and mutterings of the crowd close by; he's hidden himself away somewhere. He must be alone. What do I do next? I must get on my own, urgently, vitally. And there is David, alone with God, and I see the tears in his eyes and his heart is full. And in some way over which Scripture draws its kindly curtain, David is doing business with God.

And that's what conventions are for – doing business with God. Everything poured out to Him in prayer. Maybe all that past failure, if that's what's needed. And through the darkness the strong sense of the presence and power and love of God comes to our awareness.

'David strengthened himself in the Lord his God.' Something real happened. Something deeply personal, something totally transforming. Oh, that it might happen to us! Isn't that the prayer you've had upon your heart? And that is the prayer the loving Lord has heard.

A God in control

Let me turn to the second thought, and though it's briefer, in a real sense it is more important. For we shouldn't ever focus on man in his need without also focussing upon God and His strength. What I see here alongside this man in need is a God in control – our God in control. And though it's not at first obvious as you read through, the awareness comes to you that David is not alone in this, that God is working His purposes out for Israel as well as David, even in the darkness of that desperate situation.

God was in control, in the glorious sense of our God being the omnipotent God of the whole history of His world. And though we may not see it at present, the truth is that our God reigns. While David strengthens himself in God, therefore, this loving God has His hand upon David and is moreover in action for His own glory and honour in the world in which David lived.

Quickly turn the pages. In 29:1, the Philistines are said to be gathering all their forces at Aphek and the Israelites are camped by Jezreel. This is the background. There's going to be a battle. That battle will be traumatic, it will prove a turning point for Israel, because Saul is going to be killed.

Turn back to chapter 28. We haven't time to do more than just remind ourselves of the situation. Saul has – wholly wrongly – sought help from a witch at Endor. Scripture invariably and without apology condemns such things as wrong. Saul – what on earth are you doing? The result is that in some amazing way, I don't propose to begin to understand how, Samuel is raised up. Samuel who has died is face-to-face with Saul. And what does Samuel say? Read verse 16. Do you sense it? God is in command. God is in action behind all these strange and difficult events. Read verses 18 and 19. Surely, that word 'tomorrow' is significant? It's not just somewhere in the vague future. It's tomorrow! Just twenty-four hours from now, Saul, you're going to be dead and your sons with you. Chapter 29 and chapter 30 simply elongate the time scale, for when you turn to chapter 31 it's twenty-four hours later, the Philistines are now fighting against Israel, and this has been going on while David has been at Ziklag.

The focus of the sacred story is on David at Ziklag, but the background is this mounting battle. And what a twenty-four hours it must have been. Look at 32:2. Saul perished by his own sword. And David knew nothing of it. For he has problems of his own, and all he can see is his own problems. But God is in action; and in an amazing way He is, in those twenty-four hours, clearing the way for His purposes to be worked out in Israel.

But David knows nothing of it; that's the point; he's gone back to Ziklag, to his own problems. He will not hear, in fact, of the defeat and death of Saul and the death of his dear friend Jonathan, until the first chapter of Second Samuel – and then it comes home to him. The whole world seems to have come apart. Where is the future now? The lamentation of David over Saul and Jonathan is perhaps one of the greatest passages of English literature, just as it must be in Hebrew literature. Read it with tears. But what has happened?

In the goodness and mercy and sovereignty of God, the way has been cleared for all the future, under God's chosen servant David. In 2 Samuel 2, he moves to Hebron. Later, he moves to Jerusalem. His kingship over Israel and all the glorious days of Israel's high point in history lie in the future. Tragic though Saul and Jonathan's deaths are, and tragic though the situation is that David finds himself in at Ziklag, in fact God is in control the whole time, and is in action, although David doesn't know it. And I want to ask; who can tell what God is doing, in these days in which we live? Maybe we're so stunned by events that we don't see – as we should see as Christians – that our God reigns, that He will be exalted and that He will be seen to be God and Lord, for he is the Lord of history. And you and I need to strengthen our souls again in this Lord who is our God.

For we who come to Keswick battered, maybe, and bruised and weary – we are on the glory side, the winning side! The Lord God omnipotent reigns – and He is our God! And we can come to Him and assuredly find strength in Him. Oh, what a difference that view makes, doesn't it!

I believe that we all need, in these difficult days, to have our eyes opened wider and wider still. We need to see not just the problems, but the Lord, high and lifted up. Yes, the God who loves you, who wants so much to do business with you in love, to have mercy on you and put His strong arms of love around you, dear Christian man or woman. So that you may be strengthened in the Lord your God, for all His service.

It's interesting how the various translations link up. The New English Bible: 'he sought strength'. The New International Version: 'he found strength'. The Good News Bible: 'The Lord his God gave him courage.' He sought, he found; because God gave it.

May those words be written over our Convention! That this is a great crowd of people seeking God, and that you're going to find the Lord, and that He's going to give you the strength for all that the future may hold in store – perhaps a golden age in the history of your life. Amen! So be it.

DEMAS

by Rev Sinclair Ferguson

2 Timothy 4:9,10

The words of our passage are of course among the last known words of the Apostle Paul. He is now in prison in Rome, facing certain death. He has resigned his life and his witness into the hands of God. He knows that soon he will lay his head on the executioner's block and that his soul will be brought into the presence of God, and that he will see there the face of the one he has served for so many years. And yet, as he writes to possibly his dearest friend, alongside the testimony that he has fought the fight and kept the faith and run the race and finished the course, he also pens what has become for us not his own epitaph but the epitaph of another dear friend. And in that epitaph he summarises nearly all that we know of that friend's life. 'Come to me quickly, Timothy, for Demas has forsaken me. He has gone to Thessalonica because of love for this present world.'

I suppose that there are very few characters who surrounded Paul and shared in his ministry, about whom we know less than his companion Demas. He is I think mentioned only twice elsewhere in the New Testament – towards the end of the letter to the Colossians and towards the end of the letter to Philemon. We know very little more about him than what we read in these verses in 2 Timothy. And what we read in these verses is undoubtedly one of the greatest and most tragic lapses of a professing servant of God about whom the New Testament speaks.

We do not know very much about him, but perhaps the most striking thing we do not know is whether his lapse was temporary or permanent. You may remember, in *Pilgrim's Progress*, Bunyan says, 'I saw that there was a way to hell, even from the gates of heaven.' And we just do not know, for Demas was in a very real sense near to the celestial gates. He was Paul's companion; and it was as though the very angels of heaven were already on their way to transport the Apostle to the other side. Demas should have been able to hear the faint echo of the heavenly voices praising Christ and magnifying His name for the grace of God in His servant Paul. And I say to you, we do not know whether he trod on that pathway which leads from the gates of the Celestial City and takes a man to final apostasy and final destruction.

But in a sense, it is unnecessary for us to know; because all that God wants to teach us through the life and sad experience of this man is summarised in the epitaph that the Apostle Paul writes for him. He is not there set forth as an object of speculation. My dear friends, he is set before us as a warning beacon, an illustration of the kind of thing that can reappear in the hearts of God's people in these days.

And I want to draw your attention to the life and epitaph of Demas as an illustration of the grave possibility of spiritual declension in a professing child – indeed, servant – of God. In all that Paul says about his erstwhile companion he summarises not only the heart of Demas, not only some of the things he knew in his own heart when he told us that he kept his body under, lest he too should prove a castaway. In these three massive, penetrating statements he makes about his former friend he tells us in a very real sense all we need to know. First, Demas has forsaken me. Second, Demas has gone to Thessalonica. Third, Demas has loved this present world. The marks of spiritual decline in a professing Christian.

Demas has forsaken me

A more accurate translation might be, 'Demas has left me in the lurch.' – Demas has abandoned me in the hour of my greatest need – when I made my pleas before Caesar nobody stood by me because Demas had forsaken me.

And in all the sense of triumph and glory and joy and expectation in the Apostle's song of praise, in the final words he speaks to God's people, there is a minor key running through the symphony of praise; that in the midst of it all, with all this to look forward to and yet with so much to suffer, one of God's professed servants has left him in the lurch. Whereas there is for him a crown of righteousness to which he looks forward, he feels the appalling loneliness of having been deserted by one of his companions. And it is very important for us to recognise this.

The Apostle is not saying – as he says of some other men in this chapter – that Demas had merely left him. If that were the case there would not necessarily have been anything wrong in it. Other men had left Paul to carry the gospel to other places. Other men had left him because they saw fresh opportunities or new needs. But none of those men had deserted Paul, had left him in the lurch. It wasn't that Demas had gone somewhere else where necessarily the going was easier and less rough than it was to prove to be in Rome in the days of the burnings and executions. But rather it was that Demas had deserted the place of God's appointment.

And we must be very clear that in these verses the Apostle is not speaking as some megalomaniac growing old in his loneliness, but as the pastor of this man's soul. And out of the depths of his pastoral concern and compassion for this man's soul, the epitaph that he writes over his life here is that of a professed servant of God who has deserted Christ's cause. There are a number of reasons for the Apostle saying such a thing. One of them is that Demas had deserted his divine calling.

The only other significant thing we know about Demas is that we are told at the end of the letter to Philemon that he was a fellow-worker with the Apostle; he was a fellow-worker with Luke the beloved physician and with John Mark; and that conjures up for us the most marvellous picture of some of God's dealings in the life of this man.

The reference to 'Thessalonica' probably means that that was the town or village of his origin where he had been brought up, and where he had been brought to Christ in those marvellous days when the Spirit of Christ had come down upon that place in awesome power and marvellous grace, and men had turned from idols to the living God and there had been a mighty awakening. And some of them, like Demas, had sensed the hand of God laid on them, distributing the gifts of the Spirit, enabling them to minister God's Word and to be servants of the Lord's people.

And as Paul had ministered in Thessalonica or elsewhere, it matters not, he had noticed how there were unusual spiritual abilities in this man Demas, and he had summoned him with a sense of destiny and privilege into the apostolic band. And the day had come when undoubtedly the church of God had lifted up holy hands and pleaded with God for Demas, that he might be mightily used in the kingdom of God. And all that privilege and all that sense of destiny now lay in shreds and tatters at the feet of the lonely Apostle, because his friend Demas had deserted the divine call.

But not only had he deserted his divine call, says the Apostle: 'Demas has deserted me.' And he doesn't speak here, let me say it again, out of pique or a spiritual grudge. Few men have been more conscious of their own sins and frailties and weaknesses than the man who penned this epistle. And yet at the same time he was conscious that God had given him a special ministry among the Lord's people; and had given him a special authority as an apostle of God. And as becomes so evident throughout his epistles, God had given him surely the largest of pastoral hearts, to care for and love the people of God – and Demas had been a special, privileged object of the Apostle's pastoral care.

He could have said of Demas, as he said of the Colossians and all others, how he had striven in prayer and in labour, with all the energy God mightily inspired within him, that he might present Demas mature in Christ before the glory of God. And for some reason, we know not why, this man who had seen the privilege of the Apostle's suffering and the Lord standing by him, who had been the recipient of endless hours of marvellous ministry and exposition and application from the lips of this chosen servant of God, who had seen something of the answer to prayer, of the glory of God and the power of the Holy Spirit coming down on men and women, and who had been drawn into the intimate companionship of this great servant of God – had deserted him. And now, in far-off Thessalonica, the thoughts that he had of the Apostle Paul were no longer the thoughts that he had once known.

And I want to say to you, my dear Christian friends, that this is something to which we need to give a great deal of attention today; because it is an increasingly evident mark of spiritual decline amongst the Lord's people, that we no longer entertain that affection and loyalty and sense of awe and affection for the servants of God, who have been used by His grace to bring us into the kingdom and to bring us along in the way of Christ.

Demas knew something of that distancing of spirit, that cynicism, that turning away; he deserted his calling; he deserted the Lord's servant.

And he deserted the place of sacrifice and suffering. Demas left me, said Paul – where? 'In the lurch'. Demas, who had stood by him before; as he began to see the impending judgement of Caesar coming over the horizon with the name of Paul written large upon it, as he saw the impending persecution that was about to overflow as the floodgates opened in the city of Rome, left the Apostle in the lurch. He would not face the tribulation and persecution and cost of going on with Christ. He was like that rocky soil where the plant grows up in abundance and joy, and receives the Word of God with gladness. And then when the noon-day sun of trials and persecution begins to emerge, it withers and fades and seems to die.

And it can hardly be that in such a great company of God's professed servants as are here at Keswick that we do not find an echoing cry in our hearts and become deeply conscious that this evidence of Demas' spiritual decline couches at our door.

Demas has gone to Thessalonica

Paul speaks not only of the evidence of Demas' spiritual decline; he speaks in the second place of its direct consequences. He summarises them in the words: 'Demas has forsaken me and gone to Thessalonica.'

Why? Well, we don't know why. It may well be, as I have suggested, that his home was there. It may have been – and some of us will know this in our own hearts – that Thessalonica rather than Rome was the place where God seemed to be blessing, and rather than exercise the patience and the waiting and the sowing of the seed, to wait upon God to raise up for Himself a testimony to His name in Rome, Thessalonica seemed a much cosier place in which to serve Christ. So he made a bee-line for Thessalonica.

But what I really want you to notice in what the Apostle says is not so much why Demas went there, but the extraordinary fact that in those difficult circumstances he was able to get to Thessalonica at all. That's the astonishing thing. What is so significant about it is that so frequently, in the life of the professing child of God, the desire to flee the place of God's calling and appointment is almost invariably followed by the opportunity to do so. And there is a catalogue of names in Scripture that bears witness to that undying tactic of Satan – that where the desire rises, the opportunity will soon follow.

For example, there was David. We are told, it was the time when kings go to war; and there was David deserting the place of God's appointment, the place of his duty, at the head of his people as the Commander of God's army, defending God's people from the marauding hosts. 'Oh God,' he cried in later life, 'Why, when I was at ease in Zion . . . why, when I was walking on the rooftop . . . Why, Oh why?' Or there is Jonah, fleeing from the Word of the Lord and looking for some opportunity to fulfill his desire; and he aimlessly goes down to the port, and he looks around the ships; and there to his great delight he finds the opportunity to flee from God and go to Tarshish. Or there is Simon Peter, weak and desiring to flee from all the cost of serving Christ – and 'Why, oh why, would there be a servant girl made to speak to me then?' – so that out of his heart and mouth, like Demas, comes the denial of the Lord Jesus Christ. And you see, it is true in a very profound sense that in the life of the Spirit, you get what you want.

Demas illustrates to us that when a man desires to turn away, he has no security with which to strengthen his soul against the onslaughts of the devil. And the immediate consequence of his spiritual decline was the opportunity to flee from Christ.

Demas has loved this present world

In many ways this is the most poignant of all the things Paul says, because in these words he emphasises not only the evidence of Demas' spiritual decline and its consequence, but also its cause.

Of course Paul is not speaking of the world around us, the cosmos in its glory and beauty, that makes us lift our hearts up to God and thank Him for his mercy towards us. He is thinking of the age in which we live, that is given over to the powers of evil and darkness. He is thinking of what he elsewhere calls 'this present evil age'. Indeed it might be better for us to translate these words, 'Demas has forsaken me because he fell in love with this age.'

And I wonder if you've noticed, as you've read these verses in the past, how carefully the Apostle chooses his expressions? How he contrasts this with the grace that God was pleased to give to him, when he was ready (as he says in verse 6) to be poured out like a drink-offering and the time of his departure was come? He had grown in grace, he had fought the good fight, finished the race, kept the faith; and there was laid up for him the crown of righteousness that the Lord had promised to give to him. 'And not for me only,' he says, 'but for all those who have fallen in love with Christ's appearing'. Paul had forsaken 'this age' for the love of Christ's appearing.

And Demas had professed to do the same. Demas had professed to look forward to the crown of righteousness that would never fade away, and he had professed and preached, and he had proclaimed to all men that he loved the age to come and the appearance of the Lord Jesus Christ. And now he had turned his back upon the crown of righteousness; and instead of loving Christ's appearing he had fallen in love with this present age.

I hardly need to tell you what it means, to fall in love. It means to become so dominated by someone, so drawn away from all that you have held tightly to yourself as the first priority in your life, that you begin to feel the tugs upon your heart that make you release your grip on all that you have previously counted vital and important and first in your life, until your hands are free to welcome and embrace the object of your love.

Something of that order had begun in Demas' life. Sin had been crouching at the door. The world in all its chameleon guises and colours had come to him, in some way, we know not what; except to say that the world came in the guises that most suited the desires lying latent in the heart of Demas. And he had begun to feel the strings of his heart being tugged towards the shape of this world and its joys, and the pleasures of this age; his grip upon the age to come had been released, and he had fallen back into the embraces of 'this age' and gone to Thessalonica.

And I say to you, the real tragedy of Demas' life was this; that neither Paul, nor we, nor Demas knew whether he was a man who had merely backslidden, or whether he was a man who had committed final apostasy. And the ultimate mystery of iniquity in the life of the professed believer is that the time comes when these two things become totally indistinguishable, except to the eye of God Himself. And Paul's pastoral heart was broken; because he didn't know where Demas was. And my dear friends, our hearts likewise are broken, are they not, because this very night we do not know where Demas is.

Except – perhaps – he is here. Are you here, Demas? Are you here? My dear friend, do you know something of this in your heart and spirit? Are you here? In His mercy God has taken you from your Thessalonica and in His amazing providence He has brought you this night to Keswick. And your name is Demas.

My friend, I have a word for you; do you see that Demas is not the only name mentioned here? There is another mentioned (verse 11), a young man called Mark. Do you know who John Mark is? He is the Demas of Paul's earlier life, the man who deserted him. I don't know how or why. I only know he was back, and he was restored. I know there is restoration for deserters, and forgiveness for deserters; and welcome in Christ for deserters! And that is why I say to you this evening, there is welcome in Christ for you, Demas. There is welcome in Christ.

> O Jesus, full of truth and grace,
>   More full of grace than I of sin;
>   Yet once again I seek Thy face.
> Open Thine arms, and take me in,
>   And freely my backslidings heal,
>   And love this faithless sinner still.

Psalm 73: 1-13

by Canon James Ayre

You know, a stranger arriving at Keswick could be forgiven for thinking he'd arrived even at the gates of heaven (except for the weather ...)! There's a kind of aura, smiles and singing and greeting each other – I sit here watching you all come in – the saints come marching in! Marvellous, absolutely marvellous, and it's a wonderful privilege to be here.

Yet I'd be surprised if privately, beneath the surface, there weren't some of you – and I'm only speaking to some of you, I don't know to whom – with serious doubts and serious questions. Have you ever asked yourself the question: Have I wasted my life becoming a Christian and serving Christ? Have you ever wondered, in your soul, is it worth it, this obedience of the faith?

John the Baptist did, you know. 'Art Thou He that should come, or do we look for another?' – have I wasted the whole of these thirty years, anticipating You?

And so have many men of God, and I must confess so have I, and I suspect so have some of you. And some of you are on the point of falling; you are unable to make any progress. 'My feet', said the psalmist Asaph, 'my feet were almost gone.' So, before Chuck Smith paints the glory, I want to paint the problem. I want to look at one or two various examples which might fit our case.

Look first at Job. Forget the 'prologue', forget the

'epilogue', forget the academic disquisition in the middle on the problem of suffering and the problem of pain; give Job back his flesh and blood and what do you get, as you read the Book of Job? You get a man, a good man, a Christian man, who for no discernible reason whatsoever first loses his wealth and then (through a terrible, terrible accident – though he doesn't know anything about Job chapter 1) he loses the whole of his family, all his children. Then, on top of all that, his health breaks down. There he is, distressed with a disgusting disease. And God? . . . why, it's too painful even to say the name of God, when that happens in such tragic circumstances. It's an offence to say 'All things work together for good to them that love God' – don't ever throw that too glibly at people who are mourning or suffering. Don't do it: because Paul, in three chapters full of sorrow, takes Romans 9, 10 and 11 to justify that text and the text that is very like it, 'Nothing can separate us from the love of God which is in Christ Jesus.'

Says the unbeliever to Paul, 'What about the Jew? God called the Jew, the Jew is God's elect, His beloved – what's happened to the Jew today? God has let him down! You're joking Paul! "Nothing can separate us from the love of God in Christ Jesus"? What about your own people?' And Paul, full of sorrow, begins this awkward three chapters in the middle of Romans to justify God's dealing. Three tear-filled chapters.

Little wonder then that Job's feet had almost gone. 'It would have been better', he said, 'if I had not been born.' A Christian man is speaking: where is God in all this?

And let me say this; that I know personally that bitterness, that cup of sorrow. I lost the sweetest, most wonderful girl in the world two years ago; and – God? I couldn't talk to God, couldn't face Him; I believed in God, but all I could say was, 'You're the Lord.' I couldn't talk to Him! It was too painful to look up and even *try* to talk to Him! I'd hide my head from God and say, 'Well, over to you; I don't understand.'

And I'd been in the ministry thirty years. *God*?

It stops one's prayers – strips faith of all fantasy – reduces it to bedrock bare necessity until you're hanging by your finger tips. Truly God is good to us, we can say; but as for me, my steps had almost gone.

Look at Elijah. Was there any man more completely given over, body, soul and spirit, to God's will than Elijah? Three years living by faith alone, one man in contention with a whole nation in its apostasy, in its coldness and blindness; convinced that he was God's man, convinced he had God's message. And then that awe-inspiring confrontation on Mount Carmel, and the marvellous vindication of the living God – 'If Baal be God, worship him; if Jehovah be God, worship Him' – (no doubts now, we say: Jesus Christ is Lord!)

And then, almost overnight, all is swept away; and the devil is back on the throne and evil is rampant; and Elijah – depressed? That isn't the word! He was in total despair: 'Let me die, let me die, let me die, I just don't understand, my feet have almost gone.' And you know there's many a Christian worker, there's many a Christian missionary, there's many an ordinary Christian believer who's found him or herself in that particular situation.

A missionary came to me a short time ago. 'Rector, I'm to go back to the field. And I've lost my love for the field, I don't want to offer these people Christ, I don't know whether I believe. What do I do? Do I go back to the field?' I said: 'You don't go back. You stay with me, and you rekindle those fires.'

My feet were *almost* gone ...

Look at the text. He was a very honest man, Asaph who wrote this song; he made public his private doubts. You read them in Psalm 73. You can't escape them, can you? They do have a marvellous time out there, says Asaph. We Christians, we're under authority, under constraint, under chastisement; but they are free, and they boast about it – their self-fulfilment, their freedom, their pleasure, their sex, their money, their lack of moral constraint. And don't think, says Asaph, that they don't die well. They *do* die well, many of them. There are no pangs in their death, no fearful anticipation. They actually look forward to dying so people can read their wills – amazing, isn't it? Worldly men – 'You know old Bill Jones has left £150,000?' And it's hard not to envy them. 'God?' they say, 'You and your God! How does God know? What does He care?'

And here am I, you say; a Christian daily hedged in by conscience and God's Word, restricted, convicted, chastised. Oh, says Asaph, have I made a mistake? Have I washed my hands in innocency, is my faith vain? And I'd be very surprised if some of you haven't thought like that, looking at your friends or even other members of your family, and if the thought hasn't sometimes shaken your faith. Isn't that true? That remarkable women Teresa of Avila once complained, 'Lord, I'm not surprised You have so few followers, the way You treat your friends.' Isn't it true?

Last of all: take Peter. 'My feet were almost gone' – you know if I'd been Peter I would have thought my feet had entirely gone for ever. He was so privileged, so near Christ, so certain, so prominent; and yet at the very time when the Lord was in desperate need of one supporting voice or one sympathetic face Peter openly and violently denied Him. The unforgiveable sin, surely; at least, I would have thought so and so must Peter have thought.

So there you are. Ask yourself, 'How do I stand, today?' Some will be facing some temptation; some of you are going to say, 'My feet are almost – almost – gone.' But 'Who is a God like unto Thee, that pardoneth iniquity, and passeth by the remnant of His heritage? He retaineth not His anger for ever, because He delighteth in mercy' (Micah 7:18). Who is a God like unto Thee? Hear me this day, O Lord; my feet have almost gone.

So what's the answer? Look again at Job, barely clinging on in his misery and darkness – and then God speaks: He lets everyone have their say at first, and after all the froth and the bubble and the crying and the righteous indignation, God speaks. And He's speaking to some of you now, in precisely the same way. What did He say to Job? 'Go out on to the hills, Job. Look around at the richness and the care and provision for man and bird and beast. Drink it all in, and think, Job – is it conceivable that God, whose heart beats at the fall of a sparrow, who designed all this magnificence, should be lacking in love and thought and sympathy for you who are made in His own image and redeemed by His own blood? Is it? Of course there are mysteries about evil, about Satan, about death – but can't you trust, in the face of all this, that I who have the whole world in my hands, have you in My heart?'

There's no argument, no explanation – just a challenge to face. And Job stood up, and he said 'I'm sorry Lord; I repent.'

Go out, look, ponder. Is it conceivable that such a God has deserted me and acted unfairly? That's the question I've got to ask myself. Was he mean, or cruel, or unfair to me when he took my wife?

Take Elijah. What marvellous condescension to an over-wrought servant of God; what kindness; there's no shouting, no rebuke, no thunderbolt, no fire, no shaking the life out of the man at all. Just the sound, the Hebrew says, of gentle stillness, a listening and a sympathetic ear: 'What dost thou here, Elijah?' (1 Kings 19:13). 'What's the trouble, Elijah – tell me, Elijah?' And Elijah did, he poured it all out. And God talked back to him; and God talks back to us if we're real and we want to listen to Him, if we want to get down to brass tacks. And He says something like this.

'It's not as bad as you think. I've got the situation under control. Don't start worrying about the Church, it can't fail, I'll see the elect home – but you, Elijah, you need in the first place a friend, you need a human friend, go and get Elisha. And secondly you need to get back to My work. And remember it's My work, not your work; and remember too to get your perspectives right, to leave the outcome with Me.'

You know we Christians think, like Elijah, that if we get rid of one evil we're bound immediately for the kingdom of heaven. We've got our perspectives wrong. Behind that evil is another, and behind that is another; that's what shook Elijah, he'd got his perspective wrong. When he'd defeated the priests of Baal he'd forgotten about Jezebel, and behind Jezebel was yet another, and another.

I worked in Israel for seven years. For the first three I went round the country, a flaming evangelist, and got nowhere. It's a hard and barren land, and it seemed to me that all the missionaries were dead, the Jews were very antagonistic, I was doing all the preaching and shouting and getting nowhere quickly. And I remember one night in Jerusalem I was to preach to a handful of people and I got down on my knees an hour before and I said: 'Lord, I'm sick to death. If you don't work in this land I will never go back to England, take a church and encourage people to go out on the mission field. Because if you can't work here you can't work anywhere.' – that was James Ayre talking to God. It's a wonder a thunderbolt didn't come through the window. It didn't. That's the extraordinary thing; I heard instead a still, small voice, a sound of gentle stillness. It came over me; I knelt; and it was as though God were speaking to me. 'Who are you to talk to Me like this, James Ayre? You get on with the work; it's My work, not your work. Just give the Word of Christ to these people; that's all you're asked to do. Go and do it.'

I got up and went into church and preached; and a woman dentist said to me, 'Mr Ayre, I could have stood on the pew tonight and clapped you when you preached.' I said, 'Really? Why?'

She said, 'I don't know why – something different ... something different.'

And from that moment I got 100 Jews in a houseparty, and the next year 110; preaching the gospel to them. The next year we couldn't get them all in – a whole week's houseparty; and because of that I was able to buy a big fellowship centre on Mount Carmel. Israel! You know, they *hate* Christians ...

A still, small voice.

And Asaph – honest Asaph – very few of us would stand up and be honest enough to say that we were envious of the wicked. But Asaph did. God loves a controversy with an honest man; and in the sanctuary, with his Bible, in his quiet time, in his prayer, Asaph saw what a fool he had been.

These careless men belonged nowhere but to uncertainty of life and to a certain, fearful judgement. Let them enjoy the pleasures they're having now – because Scripture says, that's all they will have. But you are being prepared, you are being trained for 'joy unspeakable and full of glory' (1 Peter 1:8). You are being made ready for such good things as pass man's understanding; you are eternal, you are blessed of God and you're going to inherit that not long hence. We all live very short lives. You might envy the wicked; but they'll be dead in a year's time. You know that terrible parable of Dives and Lazarus? The whole scene changes. 'Now there's a gulf fixed . . .'

But it's with Peter that I'm going to end. If I were to stand here now – just use your imagination – and if I were to deny our blessed Lord Jesus Christ, to use gutter language and curse and swear – try to imagine your reaction. Dreadful thought, isn't it? Any time you heard my name it would be with revulsion as a hypocrite and as 'that unspeakable man who used our blessed Lord's name with curses and filthy language'.

But have you ever thought of that meeting on the seashore at Galilee, between Christ and Peter? Never a word, not a word of reproach or recrimination; just this. 'Do you love Me, Peter? Do you love Me just a little? Then feed My lambs. Feed My sheep.'

That's grace. That's amazing, heartbreaking grace. That's Jesus. Ready to put up with not only the contradictions of sinners but the base ingratitude of the saints. And He's waiting for just one cry: 'Lord, help Me!'

You know sometimes in the last couple of years that's the only prayer I could pray – God was with me in the ministry but I couldn't pray. I could barely lift my head and say 'Lord, help Me!' And that, I want to say to you, is the hope and glory of the cross. Death itself was not too much for Him to suffer, to pardon and to cleanse and to restore me – death wasn't too much for Christ. Who is a God like unto Thee?

Oh, the gospel of grace! Isn't it wonderful? My feet were almost gone. I've been through the motions, I'm a dry stick,

I'm an empty vessel and what now? Will you also, says God, go away?

Well, let me ask you: to whom will you go? If you're going to leave Christ, to whom will you go?

I would ask you, as Sinclair Ferguson asked in his message on Demas: What's your name? Is it Peter? Job? Elijah? Asaph? Demas? John Mark? Let me say this: I don't care what your name is, our Lord Jesus is standing here tonight and says to every frail and doubtful and treacherous soul, 'Come back! I love you! I love you – trust Me, I will cleanse you and forgive you and set your feet once again on the Rock!'

Do it with me.

PSALM 73 : 14-28

by Rev Chuck Smith

This address was given immediately after that given by Canon James Ayre (p.174).

Inasmuch as we have had such an excellent exposition of the first half of Psalm 73, as he was speaking I felt: Well, surely; we can't end in the first half. There is an answer.

From the beginning, Satan has been seeking to cast doubt on the fairness and justice of God. In the Garden of Eden when he came to Eve, the whole insinuation was that God is not fair: 'God is trying to hold back from you something that is good; God knows that the day you eat of it you are going to be as wise as He is. God isn't fair, Eve! He is trying to keep you from something that is desirable and something that is good.' And Satan is constantly coming to us, and challenging the justice and the fairness of God.

How many times, speaking in the various universities, do I have young students come up to me afterwards, and they say: 'Yes: but if God is a God of love, how come children are starving to death in Cambodia? If God is a God of love, why do we have so many wars in the world? If God is a God of love, then why is a child born with physical deformities and has to face his entire life with a handicap?' And these are indeed difficult questions for us to respond to. For we do know that God is a God of love and that He is absolutely just and fair.

You remember Jeremiah in his twelfth chapter said, 'Lord, I know You are righteous – but I want to ask you about a few things. How come the wicked prosper? Why are they happy who deal treacherously? Now, Lord; I know You are righteous – but there are some things I don't understand.'

Now it is important, I think, that we notice that Asaph began this 73rd Psalm with that affirmation, 'I know that God is good.' It's important that we do have certain foundational things that we know that we can always fall back on, because there will be experiences of life that we do not and cannot understand, and Satan takes advantage. He takes advantage of those situations to challenge in our own minds the fairness and justice of God. God said, 'My ways are not your ways ... My ways are beyond your finding out,' and I often face difficult situations and I wonder, where is God in this? But whenever I come up against something I don't understand, it is important that I fall back on what I do understand.

I understand that God is fair; that He is just; I understand that He is righteous in all that He does; I understand that He loves me; and sometimes that's all I understand in a situation, and I cannot rationalise my position with what I know. Sometimes I too cry out, 'If God loves me, why has He allowed this to happen to me?' Satan is constantly challenging the love and justice of God, and when he comes to us with these challenges it's important that we notice that he always exaggerates the claims. Notice as Asaph goes down and talks about the wicked he is really exaggerating. 'There are no bands in their death.' Oh, that's not true, the wicked do have horrible deaths also. 'They have no trouble like other men.' That's not true; wicked men have just as much trouble as righteous people. But you see, when Satan starts playing with our mind and is building a case there's always that exaggeration. We see the situation worse than it really is. But we with Asaph find that our feet almost slip, in fact Asaph declares in verse 16, 'When I sought to know, to understand this, it was too painful for me, I just couldn't handle it. I sought to figure it out, but it was just too painful for me.'

Then is there no answer? Oh yes, there is; let us go on to the next verse – 'Until I went into the sanctuary of God, and then

I understood their end.' Our problem is that Satan always creates a near-sightedness with us, we are looking always only at the immediate, we forget the long-term. We get near-sighted; as Peter said, 'They cannot see that which is afar off.' We find that true so often in our own cases, we lose sight of the eternal and we get caught in this temporal realm. And yet Paul said, 'We look not at things which are seen. They are temporal, but we look at the things which are not seen, for they are eternal.' But when we get our eyes off the eternal and we begin to look around at the temporal, it is all too easy to get tripped up in our own judgement, in our thinking, in our evaluation of God. Oh how valuable it is to go into the sanctuary of God, just to get our perspective of life again.

And how many times do we find ourselves coming into the sanctuary of God beaten and battered by our experience of the world out there, our feet almost slipped and just filled with pain? As I look at a world that is suffering, in such great need, I think: O God, what can I do? And I have been facing all these problems of the world for which I have no answers, and I just come crawling, sometimes, into the House of God, praying 'God, help me to get there!' But as I come in and God begins to minister His eternal truth and His Word to my heart, suddenly I get a true perspective on life. I see things in their true light.

And thus Asaph goes on to speak of the new sight that he has, coming from being in the sanctuary of God. 'The wicked of whom I was envious – Oh, they are walking on slippery places, God is going to cast them down to destruction, how could I be envious of them? Oh God, how could I have been so foolish in my accusations of You? How could I have been so foolish in my attitudes, my anger? My heart was grieved ... Oh so foolish was I and so ignorant.'

For there in the sanctuary, he began to realise all that he had. And oh that tonight we could realise all that we have in Christ Jesus; if God, by His Holy Spirit, would only open up our hearts to understand all that God is and wants to be to us. He begins to describe the blessings that are his. First – 'I am continually with thee.' God is with me in every situation and circumstance of my life! A few years ago, several people were moving out of California because people had had visions that it was going to separate off and slide into the Pacific Ocean. Somebody said to me, 'Are you going to move?'

I said, 'Oh, no.'

'Yes, but what if it slips off into the sea?'

I said, 'Well, I hope my surf board will be handy – I'll get a good ride ...'

'But aren't you afraid?'

'Oh, no,' I said. 'David said, "The Lord is my refuge and my strength; I will not fear though the mountains be removed and cast into the midst of the sea." '

God is always with me, the Lord is on my side! We need to become more conscious of the presence of God. I think we sometimes make a mistake in thinking of Him as limited to a locality. You remember the story of Jonah? He was trying to flee from the presence of the Lord. So often we think of God as dwelling in this tent, or in the church, and we so often hear prayers – 'Lord, we are so glad to come into Your presence this morning' – 'It is so good to gather in Thy presence.' Oh yes; but listen – you were in the presence of God when you stumbled out of bed this morning! When you were going over to get your clothes on, the Lord was there! That was the glorious revelation in Ezekiel – *Jehovah-shammah* – the Lord is there, even in Babylon, even in the place of captivity and exile. And we need to become conscious of the prevailing presence of God just as David was in Psalm 139: 'Where can I flee from Thy presence, Oh Lord?'; just as Paul was when he said to the epicurean philosophers on Mars Hill – 'In Him we live and move and have our being.' If only we were more conscious of this we wouldn't need so many sermons on holiness; because there is nothing that causes me to be careful of what I do more that the realisation that I am living, I am moving, in the presence of God. He surrounds me at all times. I cannot escape Him: 'I am continually with thee.'

The second blessing: 'And you hold me by my right hand.' People often say, 'Just hold on to the Lord, brother; just hold on to the Lord.' Well, I am grateful that my relationship isn't so tenuous that I am holding on to Him. When I take my grandchild for a walk and we come to a road, I don't say, 'Hold on to Grandpa,' I say 'Let Grandpa hold on to your hand.' For you see if a danger arose, and I went to move them quickly, their grip might be loosened, they could be hurt; but if I am holding them they are held by my strength. I have the capacity to pull them out of danger. With God holding onto my hand, He has the capacity; Oh the joy, that God holds on to me!

And the next blessing that he sees – verse 24 – 'And Thou shalt guide me with Thy counsel.' How often, how often I come to God and say, 'Lord, show me Your way, I will frankly admit to You my own ignorance.' But that's not a bad thing; Asaph admitted his – 'So ignorant was I and so foolish.' I have made so many mistakes; I have come to the place of mistrusting my own judgement, I have come to the place where I realise I had better not make a judgement in the most obvious situations, I'd better seek the guidance of the Lord.

You remember when Joshua was leading the Children of Israel in the conquest of the land, and they had the history of Jericho; and of course, confident in the victory of the flesh they went to Ai without the guidance of the Lord, and they were defeated, but then with God's guidance they went again to Ai; and they were able to defeat them. And then along came the Gibeonites with their mouldy bread and worn out clothes and they said, 'We have travelled a long way, this bread was hot in our hands when we left home, these shoes were new on our feet, we've come a long way and we're going to make a treaty with you. Because your fame has spread so far, of how God is with you.'

And notice, they took not counsel, they did not enquire of the Lord, but they took stock of their victuals. They looked at the mouldy bread and the worn out clothes and they said, 'We don't need to ask God about this; it's quite obvious these men have come a long way. Making a treaty with them out there won't make any difference.' And they were drawn into an alliance with these people, of whom God said 'Make no treaty with the people within the land.' It was because they took stock of their vituals, and didn't enquire of the Lord. Even that which seems so often obviously right to us is many times wrong, as we measure it with our own understanding. But the beautiful thing is that God is willing to guide our lives if we will but ask.

James said: 'You have not, because you ask not.' How many mistakes I have made, using my own judgement, not enquiring of the Lord until it's all over; and then I, with Joshua after Ai, get on my knees – 'Oh God, why are you allowing this to happen to me?' God usually says, 'Stand on your feet; what's wrong with you? If you'd prayed first you wouldn't be in the mess you're in.' (When I've made these foolish mistakes I don't usually get much sympathy from God!) Oh, but God will guide by His counsel, He is with us, He will hold us by the right hand, He'll guide us – Oh, my! And I was envious of those foolish, wicked people who are heading for destruction!

But one more thing. All this – and heaven too. Through my life God will never leave me nor forsake me; through my life He will lead me by my right hand; through my life God will guide me with His counsel – and then, when it's all over, He will 'afterward receive me to glory.'

If I did not know that God was working, if I did not know that God had a plan, I would be off somewhere in a little hideout and I would be stocked up with supplies and guns to protect myself and I'd be just waiting for the end of the world. The world is in a mess, and it's not getting any better; but thank God, as a child of God, no matter what may happen in the world about me, I will not fear; the Lord is with me. 'Yea though I walk through the valley of the shadow of death I will fear no evil, for Thou art with me' – He's holding me by the hand; and one day He's going to lead me into glory.

And so Asaph ends his psalm: 'Who have I in heaven but

Thee? ... though my flesh and my heart fail God is the strength of my heart and my portion for ever, for lo those who are far from Thee shall perish ...' Yes, Satan can bring us to the place where our feet are almost slipping; he can bring us to the point of hopelessness and despair; he can bring us to that point when we're almost ready to give up. But oh, thank God that there is an answer for every child of God! And coming into this sanctuary, God broadens our views and we see that He is on the throne. He rules over all. And if you'll just allow Him, He'll hold you by the right hand; if you'll just seek Him He will guide you with His counsel, and He will receive you into glory. Envious of the wicked? Oh no, you see, it all depends on the light in which you look.

Consider David. If you were standing there with the armies of Israel, you'd say 'Oh! That poor little boy going out against that big giant – that's not fair!' But you remember David, as he faced the giant, said 'You come after me with a sword and a spear – but I come against you in the name of the living God.' And if you could see that scene from the other perspective, you'd say: 'Oh, that poor little giant, going against David's living God! He doesn't stand a chance . . .'

You see it's the perspective in which you look at things. In the sanctuary of God my perspective is corrected. I see things in the light of eternity. And that's how I must be looking, because God is always dealing with you in the light of the eternal. His plan for you is an eternal plan. The reason why I cannot understand the present moment's distress is because I cannot yet see it in its eternal perspective; but God is working out that eternal plan always in my life, and though it may bring momentary discomfort it's worth an eternal weight of glory.

So may God, as we are in His sanctuary, correct our whole perspective; and may we see things in the eternal perspective of God. And our hearts will rejoice in all that we are and in all that we have as children of God tonight. And we can go out, and face a world that is suffering; we can face the world that is hurting; but we can help that world because now we are looking at it from the right perspective. And rather than despairing, we have a message of hope for an otherwise hopeless world.

KESWICK CONVENTION 1981

List of tape numbers for addresses included in this book:

These tapes can be obtained, together with a full list of Keswick tapes, from:

Anthony C Gill, Tape Secretary
Keswick Convention Tape Library
13 Lismore Road
Eastbourne
East Sussex BN21 3BA